BLACK & WHITE

Living life according to plan

Kevin Simpson

BLACK & WHITE - Living life according to plan

www.wearenotgod.com

ISBN-13: 978-1512143119 ISBN-10: 1512143111

Congratulations!

You have just taken one of the wisest, most crucial and essential steps you will ever take in your lifetime.

From this day forward, if you follow through, you will begin to watch with amazement as your destructive habits and hang-ups fade to mere challenges…no matter what they are.

From this day forward, you will begin to see the world as it really is. Although before us in living color, it will suddenly reveal its true colors; BLACK & WHITE as it should be -- once blind but now you see.

From this day forward, you will appreciate unlike any other time that a light shining as a result of absolute truth within is not the same as light shining from what is thought to be truth; you are now embarking upon absolute truth as humanly possible.

Remember! 'The mind is like a parachute…it only works when it's open!' We can close it as any fool can do --- or we can leave it open to live and learn among the wise.

FYI

This book, '**BLACK & WHITE**- Living life according to plan, is the follow-up book to 'Why Should I Believe Jesus - why not Muhammad, Confucius, or one of many Buddha's,' and the first of a new, 3-book series, entitled, '*Challenged by Default*.'

Many biblical references are from the New Living Translation, (NLT) for ease of understanding. Other references are NIV, for New International Version, KJV, for King James Version and NKJV, for New King James Version etc.

In addition, when the editing and updating process was taking place, considering said book was written approximately 12 years prior to its release, it was found that the majority of scriptural references used, in which author had come to know by heart, had changed. There is however no reason for alarm as it became evident that the recognized translations in existence (biblehub.com or biblegateway.com) were merely shaping up to reflect much needed consistency in translation accountability.

NOTE: It has been clearly substantiated that no accredited, scholarly approved translation of the Holy Bible is that of a conspiracy basis. Respectfully, **King James 'Only-ism'** is incorrect with such theories, but not that it couldn't perhaps be taken more seriously in the future.

The lack of capitalization of "satan" or "devil" is deliberate and not to be seen as grammatical errors.

BLACK & WHITE Formula

BLACK & WHITE

Living life according to plan

Change is inevitable, but change starting with self is worthy of applause… (KS)

Welcome!

It's one thing for us to plagiarize back and forth worldly wisdom but a whole different ball game when the insightful wisdom tapped into and tampered with comes from the 'One' who created all wisdom (Colossians 2:3, Proverbs 2:6, James 1:5).

This book is a simple black & white illustration to inspire, motivate and encourage its readers to consider the countless benefits of living out their lives by way of absolute truth, as humanly possible, without bias or judgment, beyond the created and onto the Creator.

Perhaps this is your first introduction to God, His wisdom and His son, Jesus Christ. If so, God is already preparing to shower His blessings upon you as you begin to follow His specific plan and purpose for your life.

Maybe you have been backsliding in your walk with God and looking to re-group. If so, God is already rejoicing in your restoration.

Possibly you are rebounding from a major setback, and desperate for that breath of fresh air. If so, God is already admiring your courage and celebrating your comeback.

BLACK & WHITE

Living life according to plan

Change is inevitable, but change starting with self is worthy of applause… (KS)

From personal experience, if we're willing to acknowledge our weaknesses, God will turn them into strengths. Our new zeal for life from the moment we see what God has planned for us is difficult to restrain. Worries, fears and doubts quickly lose their destructive ability and become mere challenges; and challenges they are. An undeniable sense of empowerment overwhelms us, evident only as the work of God, the Creator, and not that, which was created.

Me the Sinner!

Hi! I'm Kevin your author and sinner. Let me first share that I am just an everyday person of average intelligence. I am no English major, I read slower than most, memory is one of my weakest gifts, and I'm humble as a result of being humbled a time or two; OK, three or more!

My upbringing was not a Christian one. We had values, rules, respect for others and property etc., but all the goodness in the world does not and will not keep you or I from the sinful nature that destroys the joy God intended for each of us to have in life. Having joy in life in general is not the same as having joy with peace in and with God ... "For all have sinned and fall short of the glory of God" (Romans 3:23).

My first introduction to Jesus Christ was through a book entitled, "The Power of Positive Thinking," by Norman Vincent Peale. It was a gift---all part of God's perfect timing and plan for my life.

BLACK & WHITE

Living life according to plan

Change is inevitable, but change starting with self is worthy of applause… (KS)

I left marriage #1 when my son was 8 months old; too young and no God! When asked to leave marriage #2, my daughter was 8 months old.

My past track record is a mere hint of the despicable and selfish sinful nature that is born of us all. Today I can blame no one but myself.

You are now standing at the edge of the rest of your life. Today, God is using this book to introduce Himself to you. He has a plan that only you can accomplish with your distinct and divine gifts and talents.

1 Corinthians 2:9 makes reference to Isaiah 64:4 that says, "No eye has seen, no ear has heard, and no mind has conceived what God has prepared for those who love him."

Although this is not written as a motivational book, it cannot help but be inspiring and encouraging to all who read it. I believe God is going to use its content as a 'SIMPLE' meat and potatoes example, of not only how easy it is for us to invite God into, and/or, back into our lives, but also the importance and the rewards that come from doing so.

Absolute Truth

When we read in the Holy Bible, Genesis 1:1-3a it says:
"1 In the beginning God created the heavens and the earth. 2 The earth was empty, a formless mass cloaked in darkness. And the Spirit of God was hovering over its surface. 3 Then God said."

BLACK & WHITE

Living life according to plan

Change is inevitable, but change starting with self is worthy of applause… (KS)

Do you know that there is literally not one piece of scientific or archaeological evidence available today to discredit those words? That type of evidence does not exist!

At the same time, 21st Century evidence pours in daily in support of what the bible says. As just one example, check out this site, www.answersingenesis.org.

I believe the common people of today, are so overwhelmed with cultish views and ideologies that real truth and fact are regrettably being lost in the shuffle. Too much information and too many quick-fix options have created the defeatist mindset, "Who cares!" Again, as mentioned earlier, 'having joy in life in general is not the same as having joy with peace in and with God,' and you are worth it to know that without that full understanding, your soul remains at risk, which need not be the case.

God cares! He cares about you and His world. He wants to introduce you to the good life. He wants you to live forever with Him in eternity. He wants you to see what can happen when 'absolute truth' is unveiled before your very eyes, within your very soul. I believe God is saying, "In all your ways acknowledge me, and I will direct your every step" (Proverbs 3:6).

We cannot afford to take God for granted, nor can we assume that leadership and the general public are everything that God stands for. He is the Creator, we are the Created!

BLACK & WHITE

Living life according to plan

Change is inevitable, but change starting with self is worthy of applause… (KS)

We are flesh...He is of the spirit form, other than Christ in the flesh!

In a nutshell, God disciplines those He loves (Proverbs 3:12), and He blesses those who ask for their hearts desire, in His name, with unselfish motives (James 4:3), and just because others are not willing to listen and learn and be obedient to a sound, fair, all loving, holy, righteous and forgiving God, does not mean, we too will choose the same path of disobedience as they have done, and live as they do as a result!

Saving the soul is easy and comparable to making a KISS Principle choice; be obedient, serving our loving Creator...or...be disobedient, pretending to know God, while serving the world and its selfish motives; thus, we reap according to the choices we make...perfectly fair!

We are all unique and distinct, with our own God-stamped, DNA, with every hair on our head numbered to prove it (Matthew 10:30), while being knit in our mother's womb (Psalm 139:13), purposely, that comes with a personal guarantee from God Himself, who promises us a future hope and plan for our lives (Jeremiah 29:11), that is built on rock...the true cornerstone of life (Ephesians 2:20).

World's View/God's View

Briefly, let's see what the world stands for and what God stands for.

BLACK & WHITE

Living life according to plan

Change is inevitable, but change starting with self is worthy of applause… (KS)

The world teaches, "do unto others before they do unto you … and **God teaches** in Luke 6:31, "Do to others as you would have them do to you."

The world says greatness is about who's on top … and **God says**, greatness is the one who serves the best…Luke 22:26 "But among you, those who are the greatest should take the lowest rank, and the leader should be like a servant.

While the world is built on hatred, jealousy, gossip, selfish ambition, greed and violence…God builds on, "love, joy, peace, patience, kindness, goodness, faithfulness, gentleness and self-control" Galatians 5:22,23.; note that this caliber of teaching alone is not collectively found in man-made religious materials...nowhere!

So it's logical to assume that God is worthy of our attention!

Does Evil Exist?

If "evil" does not exist, why is it that ever since Madeline Murray O'Hare (*who was found murdered*), insisted and achieved at having prayer removed from our school systems? And then someone added that we better not read the Bible in schools, (*the book that teaches we shall not kill, shall not steal, and love your neighbor as yourself*), while schools have become inundated with theft, belittling gossip, and wide open to killing rampages, with the latter escalating terribly?

BLACK & WHITE

Living life according to plan

Change is inevitable, but change starting with self is worthy of applause… (KS)

If "evil" does not exist, why is it that ever since Dr. Benjamin Spock who headed up the, "*We shouldn't spank our children when they misbehave*," campaign, do we have record high low self-esteem and suicides among our teens? (*Dr. Spock's son committed suicide*) … Proverbs 23:13 says: "Don't fail to correct your children. They won't die if you spank them."

If "evil" does not exist, why is it that the dignity and privacy of our children has been replaced by 'nude photos' (Child Pornography), sent via the Internet and magazines and recognized not too long ago by the British Columbia Government, as 'ART'?

My friends, you get the picture! If God didn't feel the need to put the Bible in our schools it wouldn't have ended up there in the first place.

If God didn't feel His children were worthy enough to be disciplined (spanked), He would have made us all dumber than sheep.

And if God had of felt it appropriate to exploit His children's dignity, He wouldn't have written in 1 Corinthians 13:11, "When I was a child, I talked like a child; I thought like a child, I reasoned like a child. When I became a man, I put childish ways behind me."… We might gather from this that adults are to know better than to exploit His/our children!

Now God is asking you and I in Ezekiel 18:25
"Am I the one not doing what's right, or is it you?"?

BLACK & WHITE

Living life according to plan

Change is inevitable, but change starting with self is worthy of applause… (KS)

Are you beginning to sense the difference of how the World thinks, how God thinks, and if evil really exists?

The exciting thing is, by using these simple comparisons, it becomes crystal clear of how good God is, and how evil the world is. No convincing need be done. Falsehood sticks out like a sore thumb! Only Jesus Christ can replace the evil within us, with the absolute truth, peace, and love of His intentions. Evil is the absence of God.

How Big & Powerful is Our God?

We desperately need to appreciate how BIG and POWERFUL our God, the Creator of all things, truly is.

HE is **OMNISCIENT**…infinite knowledge and wisdom. John 16:30 says: "Now we can see that you know all things."

HE is **OMNIPRESENT**…universal presence; present in all places at the same time. Matthew 28:20 says: "Surely I am with you always, to the very end of the age."

HE is **OMNIPOTENT**…unlimited power and authority. Matthew 28:18 says: "All authority in Heaven and on earth has been given to me."

Change is inevitable, but change starting with self is worthy of applause… (KS)

This very same, awesome God, the Creator of you, me, everyone and everything as we know it to be, including all wisdom (Colossians 2:3), is inviting you right now, to open your heart and let Him in. He has big and exciting plans for you, your family and business. Matthew 7:7-8, "Ask and it will be given to you; seek and you will find; knock and the door will be opened to you. For everyone who asks receives; he who seeks finds; and to him who knocks, the door will be opened."

To further substantiate God's trustworthiness and intent, He wants you to know that He divinely designed your uniqueness, your potential and your creative flair for your enjoyment, all to His glory. He notices, wants and needs you. He appreciates, loves and respects you, for who you are---you are extremely important to Him.

How Important Are You to God?

God says in Matthew 10:30, "The very hairs on your head are all numbered".

He says in Jeremiah 1:5, "I knew you before I formed you in your mother's womb."

He says in Jeremiah 29:11, "For I know the plans I have for you, plans to prosper you and not to harm you, plans to give you hope and a future."

He says in Joshua 1:5 "I will never leave you nor forsake you."

BLACK & WHITE

Living life according to plan

Change is inevitable, but change starting with self is worthy of applause… (KS)

Recap!

God took me, your author, an everyday person, of average intelligence, and as a result of my obedience, and in His grace, delivered this book as well as my previous release (**Why Should I Believe Jesus**), and the two others to fulfill this 3-book series, and He has great and bigger plans for you, and with Him all things are possible (Philippians 4:13).

He has shown you clearly what the World (satan) stands for and what He (God) stands for.

He has demonstrated how 'satan' uses common folk to accomplish his worldly 'evil' objectives. [*No Bible in schools---don't discipline our children---exploit our children as sexual objects]*

He is boldly asking us to review the facts; "Am I the one not doing what's right, or is it you"?

He is of infinite knowledge and wisdom…
He is everywhere all the time…
He has unlimited power and authority in heaven and on earth.
He numbered the hairs on our heads…
He planned for our arrival before conception in our mother's womb…
He has a plan and a future hope for our lives…
He promises to never leave us nor forsake us…

BLACK & WHITE

Living life according to plan

Change is inevitable, but change starting with self is worthy of applause… (KS)

Can religion touch this? Are you sensing the tingle making its way up the back of your neck as you read this stuff? **Read the bible itself**!

Imagine, swapping ideas with the President/CEO of the Universe; not religion and man, and his ideas of wisdom and heaven, and of being happy while forfeiting our souls! We're talking **conversations with 'The One' who created it all**!

Today is the day you can make that ultimate connection with the power source beyond all human comprehension and explanation.

Although brief, I trust the introduction you have just witnessed, has more than sparked your curiosity.

What you believe or understand at this stage is not a concern. The issue at hand is that you are humble and willing enough to take a few steps, a new leap-of-faith, trusting in the scriptural content and references used to help lead you into new, life-changing territory, and if honest, more likely than not, with a strange sense of conviction that this is the direction you should and need to take.

My desire, is for you to see why you are worth it, why your family is worth it, perhaps why your business is worth it, and why this world in its predicament of moral decline, is also worth it…so that tomorrow you can begin to walk in the truth, integrity and wisdom of the living God...and no longer in the paths of falsehood...the very place the devil wants you.

BLACK & WHITE

Living life according to plan

> Change is inevitable, but change starting with self is worthy of applause… (KS)

No human being could ever learn all there is to know about God, heaven, Jesus Christ, or the Holy Spirit. But as we trust to honor His will for us, and learn to walk in faith, while expecting His blessings and protection in return for our obedience, He will also in turn provide millions who are grateful and willing to provide personal testimony.

So my friends, read on and persevere. Take the challenge and fight the good fight. Choose to walk in the integrity, truth, wisdom, knowledge and understanding of Jesus Christ, the Son of God, the Creator of all things, who continues to fulfill promise after promise, and will continue doing so until His glorious return…DON'T BE DECEIVED by falsehood…THE FACTS ARE ALIVE AND KICKING!

So where do we go from here? Glad you asked!

BLACK & WHITE

Living life according to plan

Change is inevitable, but change starting with self is worthy of applause… (KS)

The Full Course Meal

Y/ O/ U/ A/ R/ E/ W/ O/ R/ T/ H/ I/ T/

Y/oke…we live and learn from the yoke of God
O/verseer…we live with the gift of an overseer
U/nity…we live in unity with all men

A/bstain…we live abstaining from all unrighteousness
R/epent…we live in righteousness through repentance
E/dify…we live to edify others of the grace and love of God

W/ork…we live, work and do all things as unto Him
O/bey…we live to obey honest correction and rebuke
R/ejoice…we live to rejoice in our freedom and peace of mind
T/ithe…we live to give (tithe) in furthering His absolute truth
H/umble…we live in humbleness at all times, void of pride

I/nheritance…we live in His inheritance, which is also ours
T/hanksgiving…we live to give thanks for all things in Christ's name

Y = Yoke---Chapter 1

Take my 'Yoke' upon you and learn. Matthew 11:29 (NIV)
It's our choice… the 'Yoke' of good or of evil. (KS)

From Webster's 1828 dictionary, we discover the meaning for 'Yoke', is described as follows:

1. A piece of timber, hollowed or made curving near each end, and fitted with bows for receiving the necks of oxen; by which means two are connected for drawing. From a ring or hook in the bow, a chain extends to the thing to be drawn, or to the 'Yoke' of another pair of oxen behind.

2. A mark of servitude; slavery; bondage.

3. A chain; a link; a bond of connection; as the yoke of marriage.

4. A couple; a pair; as a 'Yoke' of oxen.

5. Service.

God is saying to you and I, "Take my 'Yoke' upon you? Learn from me. Marry into my wisdom…Partner with me. I am everything and all you will ever need. You can do all things through me who gives you your strength. I give you freedom of choice to believe in me or not to believe in me. I am jealous but I am forgiving also. Come to me and I will give you rest. Give me your burdens and I will make them light. I created you on purpose with a hope and a future plan in mind. I love you.

BLACK & WHITE

Living life according to plan

Y = Yoke---Chapter 1

Take my 'Yoke' upon you and learn. Matthew 11:29 (NIV)

It's our choice… the 'Yoke' of good or of evil. (KS)

When I think of God using the word 'Yoke', I cannot help but think of the word 'vindicate' while sharing, 'Laugh where we must, be candid where we can, but vindicate the ways of God to man.'

VIN'DICATE means:
To defend; to justify; to support or maintain as true or correct, against denial, censure or objections.

To assert; to defend with success; to maintain; to prove to be just or valid; as, to vindicate a claim or title.

God will vindicate His claim to us as Lord of Lords and King of Kings, the Alpha and the Omega, the beginning and the end.

Paul says in Philippians 2:10-11: "so that at the name of Jesus every knee will bow, in heaven and on earth and under the earth, and every tongue will confess that Jesus Christ is Lord, to the glory of God the Father."
God is looking for our humbleness…then He will bless us. Proverbs 3:9, 10, says, "Honor the Lord (me) with your wealth and with the best part of everything your land produces. Then he (I) will fill your barns with grain, and your vats will overflow with the finest wine."

In Malachi 3:10, God says, "Test me in this and see that I will not throw open the floodgates of heaven and pour out so much blessing that you will not have room enough for it."

BLACK & WHITE

Living life according to plan

Y = Yoke---Chapter 1

Take my 'Yoke' upon you and learn. Matthew 11:29 (NIV)

It's our choice… the 'Yoke' of good or of evil. (KS)

Are you familiar with the expression, "Dumb as an Ox"? A farmer must 'Yoke' his Oxen before they will do what they are told to do.

With us, God is using 'Yoke', metaphorically. He is not speaking of us as animals or to literally 'Yoke' us like an ox. He is attempting to encourage us to take His 'Yoke' as in allowing Him to lead our lives.

Many will fail to accept God's grace, claiming we cannot prove that He is real. But let us ask ourselves? When was the last time the sun lost its heat? When was the last time the birds forgot their tune? When was the last time you came across the same fingerprint as your own? When was the last time the Pacific Ocean dried up? When was the last time, daylight never returned? When was the last time gravity left us hanging?

I think of the story about a mother who was praying daily for her son's salvation, in hopes that he would see the way of Jesus Christ before heading off to war. He never did make the decision before leaving and it wasn't until a life or death incident from the trenches that caused him to reconsider what his mother had always preached to him over the years… "*Son, if you invite Jesus into your heart as your personal Lord and Savior, only to find out on your death bed it was all a hoax, then you have lost nothing. If you don't invite Christ into your heart and die, finding out it was not a hoax, you've lost everything*." Hmmm???

Y = Yoke---Chapter 1

Take my 'Yoke' upon you and learn. Matthew 11:29 (NIV)
It's our choice… the 'Yoke' of good or of evil. (KS)

This mother, nor I, is able to convince you of anything, no matter our efforts. Our job is to share the good news, plant the seed, in the unique and specific means provided each of us by the grace of God. As distinct as our fingerprint is from all others on planet earth, so is our means to deliver the message of hope—same message, different personality, different delivery with a different result; all according to His perfect timing and plan.

In John 6:44 & John 6:65, Jesus says, "For people can't come to me unless the Father who sent me draws them to me." Then He said, "That is what I meant when I said that people can't come to me unless the Father brings them to me."

I believe today is that day for you, and Jesus is knocking on your door with this book. There's a time for the Creator, and for the created. Jesus says, "Take my 'Yoke' upon you and learn." Matthew 11:29

If you wanted to be in the computer business and Bill Gates offered to personally teach you for free, would you accept?

If Sydney Crosby offered to personally and privately teach your children the skills of hockey, for free, would you accept?

Well today, right now, God, the creator of the above two individuals, all their gifts and talents, every other human being and all in existence today, is offering you His wisdom, knowledge and understanding for free; will you accept?

The question to ask is, "Does wisdom chase after those yoked with the created or the Creator? Will we be bound to darkness or to light? This shouldn't be a tough decision!

In 2 Corinthians 6:14, 15 we read, "How can goodness be a partner (yoked) with wickedness? How can light live (be yoked) with darkness? What harmony can there be between Christ and the Devil? How can a believer be a partner (yoked) with an unbeliever?"

Godly wisdom and worldly wisdom are not in sync.

God carries with His promises, eternal value, and the world carries with it, temporal value, only; what good is the latter? There has to be a huge difference in being able to rest in contentment, knowing that life as we know it today, is just the beginning, compared to, not knowing anything about tomorrow (Heaven or not), and wondering if Hades (Hell), is anything at all to what the Holy Bible describes it to be—and if it is, what comfort can there be in such hopelessness?

If God is promising to provide all our needs, food, clothing, and contentment, is it not foolishness and illogical not to take Him up on it? I'd say so! [We do not have for we do not ask God…James 4:2]

BLACK & WHITE

Living life according to plan

Y = Yoke---Chapter 1

Take my 'Yoke' upon you and learn. Matthew 11:29 (NIV)

It's our choice… the 'Yoke' of good or of evil. (KS)

Look at it this way—the world discourages; God encourages! The world takes away; God provides! The world secures false hope and dreams; Heaven secures our eternity.

I cannot encourage you enough, that when God says, "Take my 'yoke' upon you and learn, then," just do it. Trust Him! We human beings will let you down (created), right, but God (Creator/Divine), will not.

When we invite God into our lives, Debts are rescued; relationships restored, decisions made wiser, anger destroyed, addictions defeated, friendships rekindled, disciplines re-focused, studies directed, families re-united, paths made clear, marriages reconciled, and peace becomes priority.

I spent twenty plus years chasing what I thought I always wanted in life, only to get there, wondering, why I ever wanted it in the first place.

Proverbs 2:6 "For the Lord grants wisdom! From his mouth come knowledge and understanding."

Proverbs 3:5 "Trust in the Lord with all your heart; do not depend on your own understanding."

Proverbs 8:18 "Unending riches, honor, wealth, and justice are mine to distribute."

BLACK & WHITE

Living life according to plan

Y = Yoke---Chapter 1

Take my 'Yoke' upon you and learn. Matthew 11:29 (NIV)

It's our choice... the 'Yoke' of good or of evil. (KS)

Proverbs 13:20 "Whoever walks with the wise will become wise; whoever walks with fools will suffer harm."

Proverbs 20:24 "How can we understand the road we travel? It is the Lord who directs our steps."

'satan' can only steal these truths when we don't know Christ.

Are you familiar with the idea that if we were to surround ourselves with successful people and learn their ways, then we could accomplish anything in life we wanted? I followed that philosophy and my track record is nothing to boast about. Yes there will always be exceptions, and I know that we can choose to follow any path we like, however, if God is not part of those plans, we can be assured, that there will always remain that sense of 'question' in the back of our minds, not to mention, a lack of true peace.

You may recall I was not brought up in a Christian home. I never understood or heard of this higher power; this Sovereign God who supposedly loved us so much, that He sent His one and only Son to die on a cross for us. Sadly enough, God or the Bible, was never mentioned during my upbringing.

There was a time however, in order for me to play hockey, I had to have a card stamped at Sunday school to continue playing the game and it wasn't until December 25, 1966, that my grandmother (Mom's side) gave

Y = Yoke---Chapter 1
Take my 'Yoke' upon you and learn. Matthew 11:29 (NIV)
It's our choice… the 'Yoke' of good or of evil. (KS)

me a Bible as a Christmas gift. I didn't know what to do with this seemingly, fictitious book of stories, other than look at the pictures, and boast of my hero David, who apparently defeated Goliath with a sling and just one, of the five smooth stones he had picked up for the occasion.

Looking back today, trying to live without God in my life, the one who molded me in my mother's womb, is precisely, why my past track record stands the way it does today. Jesus says in John 15:5, "Apart from me, you can nothing," and I can personally testify to this on multiple cases; much failure, many lessons learned, and too many dances with the devil.

Choosing to live without God in our lives, is giving in to our sinful nature; greed, pride and lovers of self. Living for God helps us to see our sinful nature, for what it is, and grants us this indescribable peace of mind that lifts us up and out of our lowest of lows.

Do I live a perfect life following God…absolutely not!

Do I live without my share of defeat or heartaches following God…of course not...with a big time 10/4 added to that one!

Nowhere does God promise abstinence from life's problems, but rather, His unconditional love, grace and mercy, when we put Him into the driver's seat of our lives: He lives to guide our every step, with all our imperfections.

BLACK & WHITE

Living life according to plan

Y = Yoke---Chapter 1

Take my 'Yoke' upon you and learn. Matthew 11:29 (NIV)

It's our choice… the 'Yoke' of good or of evil. (KS)

The number one reason, I resorted to Matthew 11:29 (above title), was because of my past track record. I knew I was wrong. There had to be an explanation for all the mess-ups in my life…Sexually, materialistically, spiritually, physically, and financially. Something was missing. I had hit rock bottom. I had no more answers. And the one's I chose, were nothing more than quick-fix, worldly solutions, being passed down to any gullible soul desperate for answers. Unfortunately, this avenue is sucking away the very joy, God intended for 'all people's' (first for the Jew, then for the Gentile – Romans 1:16), to experience.

Remember when I said, when God is in control, debts are rescued, and disciplines refocused etcetera? This is yet another absolute truth! The moment I put God back into the drivers' seat of my life, life becomes refocused to obtain wisdom and knowledge from the Creator, and not from the created; I'm given clear and immediate vision to overall resolve.

My friend, you don't know me from Adam. And it's obvious I am not a man of renowned reputation, or powerful influence, trying to steer you down a path against your will. I am a sinner saved by grace, determined to share a message with anyone humble enough to confess that we are all persons in need of improvement, and willing to admit that our world is on a never-ending decline of ill repute and sinfulness; thanks to Eve and then Adam...I just want to slap that boy! I know, I know, I'm good!

BLACK & WHITE

Living life according to plan

Y = Yoke---Chapter 1

Take my 'Yoke' upon you and learn. Matthew 11:29 (NIV)

It's our choice… the 'Yoke' of good or of evil. (KS)

Where does one turn today to find truth and integrity? Where can one begin to find realness and honesty anymore? Where does one find a crowd not requiring obscenities, sexual content, and/or murder, to support its entertainment needs?

I once saw a political figure being bombarded by what appeared to me as a little too vindictive and convenient for the other rivals, including many from the persons own political party, who were playing both sides. Appreciating that politics will always have its own self-glorifying struggles, I still couldn't help but pick up the individual's platform of position, only to discover that everything, literally, was contrary to what was being said about them by the Media and naysayers. On top of all that, the reigning Prime Minister at the time, accused of two different scandals himself, was also making sure he got in his two cents worth; and we the public continue to soak up all this biased deception and false accusations like sponges.

Point being, God provides us unwavering and absolute truth, integrity, wisdom, knowledge and understanding, to all who ask; apart from Him, we can literally do nothing (John 15), but continue to mess up.

A few thoughts worth pondering might be this: Did man create the body, the heavens, the waters, or the birds? Man can only build on and from, what was first created by God Himself. As an example, taking into consideration the body only, who would know it better, than the one who created it?

BLACK & WHITE

Living life according to plan

Y = Yoke---Chapter 1

Take my 'Yoke' upon you and learn. Matthew 11:29 (NIV)

It's our choice… the 'Yoke' of good or of evil. (KS)

Check out these articulate tid-bits of God's creative wonders?

Did you know that a man's body is 40% muscle and a woman's is 25% muscle by divine design, on purpose?

Did you know that all men have approximately 1.5 gallons of blood and a woman has about 4/5th of a gallon, on purpose?

Did you know that all men have the XY Chromosome and women have the XX Chromosome on purpose?

Did you know that not one single individual on the face of this massive planet has the same fingerprint as you or I, and all on purpose?

Did you know that Your DNA, (Deoxyribonucleic Acid…a substance in the chromosomes of human beings that stores genetic information) is specific to you and you only on purpose?

Did you know that The Brain; with its 'Sub-Cortex', Cerebral Cortex, Right and Left Hemispheres, Frontal Lobes, Temporal Lobes, Parietal Lobes and Occipital Lobes, continues to baffle the world's most brilliant minds, and again, all on purpose?

Did you know that The Cell, is the basic unit of all living things, and can be found in varying shapes, sizes and functions, all on purpose?

Y = Yoke---Chapter 1

Take my 'Yoke' upon you and learn. Matthew 11:29 (NIV)
It's our choice… the 'Yoke' of good or of evil. (KS)

Did you know that same Cell, is made up of three different components, the Membrane, Cytoplasm, and the Nucleus [The 'Membrane' is the lining of the cell, which encloses the cell and maintains its shape.] *** [The 'Cytoplasm', "Cyto" meaning cell, contains many structures that perform what is known as Cell Division, a process called "Mitosis".] *** [The 'Nucleus' is the control centre, directing and controlling all cell activities and responsible for reproduction of other cells] and, all on purpose?

Did you know that Groups of Cells, with similar functions, combine to form four main and distinct types of 'TISSUES', called the Epithelial tissue, [nose, mouth, stomach] the Connective tissue, [bones, ligaments, cartilage] Muscle tissue [cardio, voluntary and involuntary] and Nerve tissue [receives and carries impulses to the brain and back to the body], all on purpose?

Did you know that Groups of Tissues, form together to make 'ORGANS', which either perform one or more functions themselves, on purpose? [Example; Brain, heart, liver, lungs, kidneys, skin.]

Did you know that Our Digestive System, operates as a result of several 'ORGANS' working together to perform its own specific function, all on purpose?

Did you know, that The Organism, or the individual being, (Human being) is a result of all of the above, all levels of the structure combined and interacting to form a whole (integrated) being such as you and I, and all on deliberate purpose? **AMAZING ISN'T IT**!

And now let us consider the longest, closing and deliberating question ever asked.

If God could create and plan, on purpose, 40% muscle to every man, 25% to every woman, instill 1.5 gallons of blood to all men and approximately 4/5th of a gallon to all women, creatively provide men with the XY chromosome only, and women with XX only, distinctly distinguish our fingerprints and DNA from all other human creation, implant the human computer known as the brain, to baffle the elitist of minds, uniquely set apart the intricate and complex detail of each and every cell within the human body, making it so, that a similar and balanced number of these very cells, will join in groups to form tissues, as in our muscle tissues, where two or more of them come together to make up an organ such as our brain, which in turn joins forces with several other organs to operate a system like our digestive system, and then have all the levels of structure combining and interacting with each other to form a whole, integrated being, such as you and I, why on earth would we not invite such a genius, God Himself, into the drivers' seat of our lives, considering the fact also, that He has waiting for us, as promised, His unique and specific plan, that can save us the trouble and wasted time of trying to fight this world and its ideals on our own?

WOW!

BLACK & WHITE

Living life according to plan

Y = Yoke---Chapter 1

Take my 'Yoke' upon you and learn. Matthew 11:29 (NIV)

It's our choice… the 'Yoke' of good or of evil. (KS)

We cannot begin to fathom what God has done, is doing or has in mind to do for this world and us as individuals. We haven't even skimmed the surface here, of how He has masterly created the human body, and not yet even considered the 'heavens', the 'waters', the 'birds', the 'flowers', or any other divine design element and its details found on the face and under the face of His magnificent universe.

I believe we need to give up control to be in control: to take His 'Yoke' upon us and learn from Him, who created it all.

We can continue in ignorance and denial, but the almighty God, who is Omnipotent, Omnipresent and Omniscient, has more than earned His right to be first in all things.

God says in Isaiah 46:10, "Only I can tell you what is going to happen even before it happens. Everything I plan will come to pass."
Only by the removal of God and His ideals do we witness further moral decay in our societies.

No matter how we look at it, we need God in our lives. We need a Savior to forgive and save us from our selfish desires and evil thoughts that are steering us down the path of a living hell. God says in Isaiah 45:22, "Let all the world look to me for salvation! For I am God; there is no other." And Jesus Christ, His Son, our Savior, God in the flesh, says in John 14:6, "I am the way, and the truth, and the life. No one can come to the Father except through me."

BLACK & WHITE

Living life according to plan

Y = Yoke---Chapter 1

Take my 'Yoke' upon you and learn. Matthew 11:29 (NIV)

It's our choice… the 'Yoke' of good or of evil. (KS)

We are all familiar with the song, Amazing Grace! The last line of the first verse says: "I was blind but now I see."

Until we re-connect ourselves back to our true-life source, faith in Jesus Christ, we remain blind to what is unseen and subjective only to what is seen. And God says in 2 Corinthians 4:18, "what is seen is temporary, and what is unseen is eternal".

Truthful and humble confession leads to peace of mind needed.

Each and every time I find myself falling short in life, I am quickly reminded that God has taken a backseat rather than the driver's seat. Each and every time I run into marital problems I am reminded again that God needs to be in control, not I, nor my wife, nor anyone but the Creator.

The only reason we humans continue to make unwise decisions, without divine wisdom, knowledge and understanding needed, again, is because we cannot connect with such power without Him being #1, "*for in Christ are hidden all the treasures of wisdom and knowledge*" (Colossians 2:3).

So, perhaps, when the God of absolute truth says "Take my 'Yoke' upon you and learn," as in Matthew 11:29, found in the Holy Bible, leaving still, 31,172 verses left, perhaps we should listen.

The soul remains restless until it finds its rest in God - Augustine

O = Overseer---Chapter 2

For you were like sheep going astray, but have now returned to the Shepherd and 'Overseer' of your souls. 1 Peter 2:25 (NKJV)
One God, one Messiah, one Spirit = one 'Overseer' (KS)

The Holy Bible's interpretation of an 'Overseer' is a person who watches over and takes care of others. 'Overseer' was one of the terms used for leaders in the early church.

From Webster's 1828 dictionary we discover that the meaning for 'Overseer', is described as follows,
OVERSEE'R

One who overlooks; a superintendent; a supervisor.

An officer who has the care of the poor or of one with mental challenges.

One might see a Shepherd as an 'Overseer'. Should one in the flock go missing, his priority is to search, find and rescue that lost 'one'.

SHEP'HERD

A man employed in tending, feeding and guarding sheep in the pasture.

The pastor of a parish, church or congregation; a minister of the gospel who superintends a church or parish, and provided instruction in spiritual things. God and Christ are in Scripture denominated Shepherds, as they lead, protect and govern their people, (their flock) and provide for their welfare.

BLACK & WHITE
Living life according to plan

O = Overseer---Chapter 2

For you were like sheep going astray, but have now returned to the Shepherd and 'Overseer' of your souls. 1 Peter 2:25 (NKJV)
One God, one Messiah, one Spirit = one 'Overseer' (KS)

Once we 'Yoke' ourselves with God to learn, He instantaneously becomes our 'Overseer' to lead, protect and provide all our needs.

Back on page 10/11, you will recall my simple analogy of what the 'world stands for' compared to what 'God stands for!' Taking that information into consideration, wouldn't you agree that the best influence of an 'Overseer ' would be the living God, from the Holy Bible, who has our best interests already planned out?

So why do we keep sidetracking from the very path that can save us? Why would we not 'Yoke' ourselves with this 'Overseer', Jesus Christ, and experience the fruits of what He has to offer? Perhaps you're thinking, "But how do we know what is best or what is right anymore?" We don't, and never have known. It comes down to you, your values, and what you see yourself standing for.

There is a saying, "*When we stand for nothing we fall for anything.*" Simply put, consider coming to a fork in the road of life, and like Alice, from Alice in Wonderland, you ask the Cheshire cat, "Which path do I take?" It doesn't really matter, if we don't know where we want to end up. The 'Overseer' does our thinking for us, step by step, and He already has that all planned out...as we walk along in trust by faith.

BLACK & WHITE

Living life according to plan

O = Overseer---Chapter 2

For you were like sheep going astray, but have now returned to the Shepherd and 'Overseer' of your souls. 1 Peter 2:25 (NKJV)
One God, one Messiah, one Spirit = one 'Overseer' (KS)

Dear friend, more times than I can count, I have failed in life. For the first twenty-nine years of my life, I was my own Overseer, apart from Him, who was zealous to give only the best to me, and in His time.

My thoughts, are, if God didn't have a purpose for us, we wouldn't be here. I was on my way out the door of a second marriage before God woke me from my stupor of life. Other than hearing the song "Jesus loves me," a time or two, I knew nothing about the church, God, Jesus Christ or eternal life. The only church I ever attended as a child was to receive a stamp on a card, allowing me to continue playing hockey in the church athletic league before moving up. Today that very church body, does not teach the Holy Bible to be the literal, inerrant word of God. In my humble opinion, until proven otherwise, Christ is who He says He is.

As we continue this journey, you should know, I'm not one to beat around the bush regarding what needs to be said. At no time do I judge, or mean to offend anyone. However, I make no apologies for addressing that which is as factual as humanly possible, void of one piece of evidence to discredit it.

"I believe in the total inerrancy of the Holy Bible; that it is the inspired and infallible word of God. Why? First, because there is literally no other belief-system in existence that can provide the scientific and archeological evidence in support of itself like that of the Holy Bible.

O = Overseer---Chapter 2

For you were like sheep going astray, but have now returned to the Shepherd and 'Overseer' of your souls. 1 Peter 2:25 (NKJV)
One God, one Messiah, one Spirit = one 'Overseer' (KS)

Secondly, 'religion' today, is either ridiculous, full of rituals, self enlightenment and insight, and/or simply bits and pieces of what can already be found within the pages of the Holy Bible, and doctored through misunderstanding."

There is more than just accountability at stake when we choose to believe in something. What about eternity? All 'religions' like Jehovah's Witnesses, Mormonism, New Age, Islam or Buddhism proclaim, "We are the way". Should we not justify these beliefs? Should there not be proof or factual evidence of some kind to support what it is we choose to believe in, considering, our souls are at stake? Proof is everything, or used to be!

In a court of law proof is required in order for a conviction to stand up. And if that proof is not provided, two or more witnesses, that case is thrown out of court as a result of insufficient evidence.

DON'T MISS THIS ONE!
Man-made religion cannot provide you scientific and/or archaeological proof of their beliefs, because there is none. For example, according to author and former Legal Editor of the Chicago Tribune, Lee Strobel, in writing to the Smithsonian Institute (not the best source), inquiring as to whether there was any evidence supporting the claims of Mormonism, he was told in unequivocal terms, that its archaeologists see "no direct connection between the archaeology of the New World and the subject

matter of the book." So in other words no Book of Mormon city has ever been located, no Book of Mormon person, place, or nation, or name, has ever been found, no Book of Mormon artifacts, no Book of Mormon scriptures, no Book of Mormon inscriptions ...leaving nothing to demonstrate the Book of Mormon to be anything other than myth and invention by its founder, Joseph Smith.

So why on earth are thousands of people putting their trust in this so-called 'religion' when the only substantiated proof available, is that of myth? My friends it's one thing to pay $1,000,000 dollars for a piece of property, and quite another, to do so before proof the property exists.

Falsehood has been leading and teaching thousands of people over the years, nothing but 'EMPTY RELIGION' according to what God tells us in His book, the Holy Bible...with which He offers proof to back it up.

Two prominent, false religions of our day, claiming to be Christian, one calling themselves 'Elders', and the other, that promotes their own New World Translation, bible, do not believe in the 'Deity' of Christ. You are not a Christian when you deny Jesus Christ as the Son of God, God in the flesh [2 John 1:9-11/Colossians 2:9,10/1 John 2:23]. Therefore, upon death, and according to the living God's word (The Holy Bible), you are not going to heaven no matter how good you are.

BLACK & WHITE

Living life according to plan

O = Overseer---Chapter 2

For you were like sheep going astray, but have now returned to the Shepherd and 'Overseer' of your souls. 1 Peter 2:25 (NKJV)

One God, one Messiah, one Spirit = one 'Overseer' (KS)

The Holy Bible is the inspired, infallible written word of God, and He does not require the assistance of these individuals, me, you, or anyone else to rewrite His word. Three times in scripture, God sternly warns those who dare to manipulate His word (Rev 22:19/Deut 4:2/Prov 30:6).

Now since man-made 'religions' commonly teach and make reference to outlandish self created information, other than what the living God has provided us, whom should we believe; God the author of life, from the Holy Bible, or the likes of man-made fiction and mythology? We are either **100% Christian or 0% Christian**...there is no in between.

By trusting in Jesus Christ as our personal Lord and Savior we defeat death and gain eternal life. On the contrary, when you deny Christ as the Son of God, as God incarnate, you have idol/man worship resulting in nothing more than false hope...meaning temporal not eternal.

While our world is into 'Religion', 'god's', and/or ' Liberal Christianity', as for me and my house, we are into Jesus Christ, the Son of God, the 'Overseer,' whom you're encouraged to introduce yourself, and get to know. Pssst: you will never get it all perfect...or even some.

Please don't misunderstand me! I believe in God and I am a Christian. However, too loosely are the words 'Religion', 'God', or 'Christianity' used today, without the slightest belief or understanding of the cross,

BLACK & WHITE

Living life according to plan

O = Overseer---Chapter 2

For you were like sheep going astray, but have now returned to the Shepherd and 'Overseer' of your souls. 1 Peter 2:25 (NKJV)
One God, one Messiah, one Spirit = one 'Overseer' (KS)

Jesus Christ, the Trinity, or anything to do with fact or absolute truth as humanly possible. There is more evidence available of the resurrection of Jesus Christ than there is evidence of Julius Caesar ever existing.

The Latin word for 'RELIGION' is 'Religio' which means to bind or to hold. We are either bound by falsehood or fact, and the Christian faith is supported, scientifically, historically, geologically, archaeologically, mathematically, and by way of cosmology, refuting evolution.

Christianity is not about a 'RELIGION'. It's about a relationship with Jesus Christ, the Son of God, and He wants to be your 'Overseer'.
The further we get away from 'Religion' and 'falsehood' the sooner we will recognize absolute truth with the power to set us free. Anyone can believe they have a Savior...but only one Savior created you and His name is Jesus Christ.

Our world is falling apart at the seams, socially, spiritually, morally, ethically, materialistically, and with no indication of how to resolve the problem. Religion is stuck at the forefront of the majority of issues while being caught up in the dilemma of, what religion is the right religion. **I say forget religion**. There is no proof in religion but there is substantial enough proof in the Holy Bible and Jesus Christ.

There is courtroom proof in the 'Overseer'. We take Jesus Christ too lightly! In Colossians 2:3, we read that, "in Christ are hidden all the

O = Overseer---Chapter 2

For you were like sheep going astray, but have now returned to the Shepherd and 'Overseer' of your souls. 1 Peter 2:25 (NKJV)
One God, one Messiah, one Spirit = one 'Overseer' (KS)

treasures of wisdom and knowledge." Is that not a fair and logical starting place, to find answers that make sense?

We must believe that we are worth it, worthy of seeing fact over fiction and witness for ourselves the power of Jesus Christ, for self, family and business. God says in Isaiah 46:10, "*Only I can tell you what is going to happen even before it happens. Everything I plan will come to pass.*" If God says He has a plan and a future for us, then He does. God is unchanging and unlike religion, He remains Divine, not religious.

Jesus Christ, as our 'Overseer' is never going to change. He is always good, perfect, and humble. He is quick to listen, slow to speak and slow to become angry. In Romans 2:4 Paul says to us, "*Don't you realize how kind, tolerant, and patient God is with you? Or don't you care? Can't you see how kind he has been in giving you time to turn from your sin*?" … My friends, this is agape love in action; Hollywood and religion can only fabricate created love, not Creator repentant, agape love.

So what is there not to like? Jesus Christ as our 'Overseer', by way of the Holy Spirit, steers us like that of a GPS system—provable beyond expectation, scientifically, geologically, archaeologically, historically — something that no other belief/faith can provide us; 24/7, 365 days a year. He is a hands-on, 100% involved, author and teacher of life with an eternal life promise attached, all secured by faith, and not by works.

O = Overseer---Chapter 2

For you were like sheep going astray, but have now returned to the Shepherd and 'Overseer' of your souls. 1 Peter 2:25 (NKJV)
One God, one Messiah, one Spirit = one 'Overseer' (KS)

Nothing else can offer such an infinite absolute solution, let alone, ability to substantiate its claims; why do we continue to miss the simple stuff?

We're challenged to recognize that real proof is everything. We need to look for facts in all matters presented to us. We need to master the art of asking questions, so we can recognize the difference between good and evil, right and wrong, with odds, probably 1000/1, in favor of 'evil'.

As an example, many have experienced a friendly visit from a certain religion at our door! Someone who has never picked up a Holy Bible would never know said uninvited visitors were speaking anything but the truth. If we were to open up the Holy Bible, an NIV (New International Version) for example, written by forty; (40) distinct, chosen authors, inspired of God, and turned to 2 John, verse 10 & 11, we would read, "*If anyone comes to you and does not bring this teaching, do not take him into your house or welcome him. Anyone who welcomes him shares in his wicked work*" ... God speaking, not me that cults are perfect examples of walking dead men/women preaching dead empty sermons.

This is only a small sample of why we need to learn discernment when it comes to knowing what is right and what is wrong with all that crosses our path, especially dealing with questions regarding 'religion'. All the proof one needs, is found within the 31,173 verses of the Holy Bible.

BLACK & WHITE

Living life according to plan

O = Overseer---Chapter 2

For you were like sheep going astray, but have now returned to the Shepherd and 'Overseer' of your souls. 1 Peter 2:25 (NKJV)

One God, one Messiah, one Spirit = one 'Overseer' (KS)

If you should choose to continue categorizing Christianity as a religion, then please keep in mind this basic principal. THERE ARE ONLY TWO TYPES OF RELIGION…according to John MacArthur of www.gty.org:

Divine Accomplishment…God in action – the Christian Gospel where the evidence is there to support its claims.

Human Accomplishment…Man in action – man's gospel where the only proof, is that of myth and the pride of human endorsement.

You will recall me saying that most man-made 'religions' do not believe in Jesus Christ, or Him as 'Deity,' God incarnate, the Son of God. In the Holy Bible, Jesus says in John 8:18, "I am one witness, and my Father who sent me is the other." Also in John 10:30 Jesus says, "The Father and I are one."And in 1 John 2:23 Jesus says, "Anyone who denies the Son doesn't have the Father either. But anyone who confesses the Son has the Father also."

It is crystal clear from the word of God, in the above verses, that Jesus Christ is the Son of God, and when we do not believe Jesus to be whom He says He is, or as promised through prophesy in the Old Testament, then we do not have the Father either.

A cult believes and teaches contrary to what God's inspired and infallible word says in the Holy Bible, and we read in Revelation 22:18 & 19,

O = Overseer---Chapter 2

For you were like sheep going astray, but have now returned to the Shepherd and 'Overseer' of your souls. 1 Peter 2:25 (NKJV)
One God, one Messiah, one Spirit = one 'Overseer' (KS)

"If anyone adds anything to what is written here, God will add to that person the plagues described in this book. And if anyone removes any of the words of this prophetic book, God will remove that person's share in the tree of life and in the holy city that are described in this book."

Mormons, when questioned on this particular verse, replied to yours truly: "*This is only in relation to this book (Revelation) and not the entire bible*." So then the other two warnings not to manipulate God's word mean nothing, or pertain to those specific books only; **SAD**!

It does not take a PhD to understand the above verses John 8:18, 10:30, and 1 John 2:23, to be saying anything different than what we read when they are in front of us. We can believe it or not; He grants us the choice.
A cult is recognized as believing other than the full gospel, as it is found in the Holy Bible, and/or, following the leadership of one person or one person's interpretation of the Bible.

EXAMPLE:
Christian Science: follows Mary Bakie Eddy
Jehovah's Witness: follow Pastor Russell & Judge Rutherford
Mormon's: follow Joseph Smith & Brigam Young
Personally, I'd rather put my trust in forty, God inspired writers, not to mention the evidence available in support of said work.

BLACK & WHITE

Living life according to plan

O = Overseer---Chapter 2

For you were like sheep going astray, but have now returned to the Shepherd and 'Overseer' of your souls. 1 Peter 2:25 (NKJV)
One God, one Messiah, one Spirit = one 'Overseer' (KS)

There is far more reason for us to have an Overseer, to lead, guide and watch over us 24/7, 365 days a year than meets the eye. Jesus Christ fills the soul with a love and joy unimaginable. He is a light unto our path. He enables a peace of mind that builds upon a sense of patience beyond description, growing stronger with time. Jesus shows us how to be humble; how to dump anger, old habits, addictions, and how to mend broken relationships, discover our divine gifts of passion that enables us to select a career and course of study with unimaginable accuracy.

In knowing what I know today with firsthand experience , nothing should be surprising, however, God never ceases to amaze me. Repeatedly, He reaches far beyond our measly feel-good sensations, proving Himself to be everything He claims and more.

I remember praying for my Aunt Eleanor's eternal security. Before attending a family gathering, I asked God, that if He wanted me to play a part in this saving experience, then He would need to open the door. As I was about to leave this gathering, my Aunt called me over to her side and said, "I think you and I need to pray." **Divine providence**! What else? The grace of God continues to answer prayer in real time, every day of our lives.

Paul says in Romans 12:2, "*Don't copy the behavior and customs of this world, but let God transform you into a new person, by changing the way you think. Then you will know what God wants you to do and you will know how good and pleasing and perfect his will really is*."

From the day I left my first wife I sensed something more than just leaving was wrong. The day my second wife asked me to leave, once again, I had a similar feeling. When my third marriage was on the rocks, God graciously showed me real love; not from the outside in, but rather from the inside out. Only when we know what's on the inside can we truly begin to love a person for who they are on the outside.

As I edit this book, my third wife and I are in our twenty-sixth year of marriage; praise God! Abraham Maslow, a famous psychologist known for 'Maslow's Hierarchy of Needs' wrote theories explaining human behavior. He believed that each individual has a free will to choose how he/she will act throughout his/her life—each individual is responsible for his/her actions and cannot shift the blame for failures or problems to anyone else, example, parents or government—he also theorized that people are motivated by their unmet needs.

In actual fact, God created everyone equal (worldly inequities take their toll), with free will to choose to believe in Him or not. This in turn, affects our behavior throughout our lifetime; we will accept and honor corporate and moral order, acting responsibly, or we won't.

O = Overseer---Chapter 2

For you were like sheep going astray, but have now returned to the Shepherd and 'Overseer' of your souls. 1 Peter 2:25 (NKJV)
One God, one Messiah, one Spirit = one 'Overseer' (KS)

As for Maslow's theory that people are motivated by their unmet needs, although he is correct in many ways, I still feel he is missing a key point. The soul is not restless because of an empty stomach, or burglars, or a job done well or not, but rather restless for a Savior, and that being, the true God. You may recall that Augustine made the statement, "The soul remains restless until it finds its rest in God."

God is the true unmet need of man. Man needs a Savior.
1/ Yes man needs food to survive
2/ and to feel secure in his abode
3/ and to have the feeling of belonging and being loved
4/ and to experience self-esteem while being esteemed by others
5/ and the comfort of knowing that a job is well done to the best of his/her ability...

Consider the following: 'Cart before the horse or Horse before the cart?'

---1/ But let us experience the true bread of life—John 6:35 (NLT) Jesus replied, "I am the bread of life. No one who comes to me will ever be hungry again. Those who believe in me will never thirst."
---2/ Let us seek security; not just home and financial, but eternal security... 2 Corinthians 4:18 (KJV) "While we look not at the things which are seen, but at the things which are not seen: for the things which are seen are temporal; but the things which are not seen are eternal."

O = Overseer---Chapter 2

For you were like sheep going astray, but have now returned to the Shepherd and 'Overseer' of your souls. 1 Peter 2:25 (NKJV)
One God, one Messiah, one Spirit = one 'Overseer' (KS)

---3/ It is good to have a deeper understanding and appreciation for belonging and being loved--- Philippians 2:1,3,4 "1 Is there any encouragement from belonging to Christ? 3 Don't be selfish; don't live to make a good impression on others. Be humble, thinking of others as better than yourself. 4 Don't think only about your own affairs, but be interested in others, too, and what they are doing."

---4/ Self-esteem, out of sync, apart from Christ, can easily germinate into 'PRIDE', which in turn destroys all who depend on self-reliance and perseverance for lifelong survival… Luke 18:14 "For the proud will be humbled, but the humble will be honored." And so can the need for constant praise from others easily become our downfall? Let us then do in secret all deeds of giving, fasting, and/or praying etcetera—Matthew 6:18 "your Father, who knows all secrets, will reward you."

---5/ What gain is there to be constantly working for self-gratification? True self-actualization and the enjoyment of it is experienced through the fulfillment of a task or tasks with unselfish motives attached---The world tells us how it is to be and we believe it, while Hollywood steps up and proves it with its renowned sitcom 'Young and the Useless,' (restless). There is a balance and understanding of self-gratification that can only be grasped when we place **Christ our Overseer** into the driver's seat of our life.

BLACK & WHITE

Living life according to plan

O = Overseer---Chapter 2

For you were like sheep going astray, but have now returned to the Shepherd and 'Overseer' of your souls. 1 Peter 2:25 (NKJV)

One God, one Messiah, one Spirit = one 'Overseer' (KS)

Matthew 6:19-21 … 19" Don't store up treasures here on earth, where they can be eaten by moths and get rusty, and where thieves break in and steal. 20 Store your treasures in heaven, where they will never become moth-eaten or rusty and where they will be safe from thieves. 21 Wherever your treasure is, there your heart and thoughts will also be."

By no means are my intentions here to discredit the amazing brilliance of Maslow or his theories, and I mean no disrespect to Hollywood and its sitcoms, nor am I judging anyone. My objective here is to add depth to each issue so the reader can see that when God, our Overseer, is involved in our lives, motives become interestingly expanded from being selfish in nature to that which incorporates unselfish motives, graciously.

I'm in agreement with Maslow's theory, considering how North America as one mere example has adopted the, "*I'm not responsible for my actions*" attitude…adults included. Jesus Christ teaches us to be responsible, unselfish, not proud or greedy, which is uncommon and contrary to secularism and religion as a whole; *women have no worthiness other than to satisfy their husbands in many eastern faiths*.

It doesn't come any plainer than what we have just read regarding the need for an Overseer in our lives. Jesus Christ is the answer. He is the living God and not a figment of religions imagination.

BLACK & WHITE

Living life according to plan

O = Overseer---Chapter 2

For you were like sheep going astray, but have now returned to the Shepherd and 'Overseer' of your souls. 1 Peter 2:25 (NKJV)

One God, one Messiah, one Spirit = one 'Overseer' (KS)

Putting Christ to the test while jumping off a building, in deliberate defiance of the laws of gravity would not only be foolish but impractical. Walking in His shoes while sincerely inviting Him into our heart, is what I would call an act of wisdom in more ways than we could ever know.

When the world courts are constantly prioritizing the criminal before the victim…or a lawyer persuading a Judge that child pornography is 'art'…or an attorney establishing the fact that rights need to take precedence even though the right in question is wrong…or supporting Prime Ministers and Presidents who insult our intelligence and defame our countries by deliberately lying on live, public television, or when churches are endorsing the acts of sodomy, and/or stealing behind closed doors from the 'One' they claim belief, then that to me is a pretty clear indicator that we are in desperate need of repentance and that it's time for an Overseer by the name of Jesus Christ to take control.

1 John 1:9 reads: "But if we confess our sins to him, he is faithful and just to forgive us and to cleanse us from every wrong." Amen!

Amen to the Overseer!

U = Unity---Chapter 3

Behold, how good and how pleasant it is for brethren to dwell together in 'Unity'! Psalm 133:1 (KJV)

Let us choose 'Unity' over envy and jealousy. (KS)

Webster's 1828 dictionary describes 'Unity' as follows:

Unity of faith is an equal belief of the same truths of God, and possession of the grace of faith in like form and degree.

Unity of spirit is the oneness which subsists between Christ and his saints, by which the same spirit dwells in both, and both have the same disposition and aims; and it is the oneness of Christians among themselves, united under the same head, having the same spirit dwelling in them, and possessing the same graces, faith, love & hope.

The minute we take on the 'Yoke' of God, accepting Jesus Christ as our personal Lord and Savior, He instantaneously, becomes our Overseer, our provider, our 24/7-365 day a year protector, for the rest of our lives…and as a result of this undeserving gift of grace, in addition, we receive the ability to humbly and respectfully live in 'Unity' with all persons, void of such things as envy, jealousy, covetousness and hatred to name a few.

Colossians 3:12 & 14 (NIV) says…12 "Therefore, as God's chosen people, holy and dearly loved, clothe yourselves with compassion, kindness, humility, gentleness and patience. 14 And over all these virtues put on love, which binds them all together in perfect 'Unity'."

U = Unity---Chapter 3

Behold, how good and how pleasant it is for brethren to dwell together in 'Unity'! Psalm 133:1 (KJV)

Let us choose 'Unity' over envy and jealousy. (KS)

So now, by the grace of God, the process of transformation begins to steer us from the way of the world and its sinful nature, to that of the living God, Creator of all things, living in 'Unity' and harmony with our fellow man, no matter race, color, creed or nationality.

God's intended objective will come to pass; having all persons appreciating the distinct and personalized chemistries that make up our unique and specific individual characters, our DNA, allowing 'Unity' to envelope the relationship at hand.

It becomes clear then, that apart from God, we are unable to live in 'Unity' with others, with exceptions of course, because we are all born sinners…and Jesus Christ died to free us from that sin. Romans 3:23 says, "For all have sinned and fall short of the glory of God" and 1 Corinthians 15:3 says," Christ died for our sins."

Until we are reconciled back with God by way of 'The Bridge,' Jesus Christ, we remain hopelessly lost and unable to neither accomplish nor discover God's good, pleasing and perfect will for us; not me, but God says this in Romans 12:2.

Many may be thinking, "But I am doing fine, I have no worries, fears or doubts, I have money in the bank, I have a good job, I'm happily married and I have many talents and friends, so what more do I need?"

BLACK & WHITE

Living life according to plan

U = Unity---Chapter 3

Behold, how good and how pleasant it is for brethren to dwell together in 'Unity'! Psalm 133:1 (KJV)

Let us choose 'Unity' over envy and jealousy. (KS)

I'd encourage you to ask yourself, who gave you your health…your ability to create wealth (Deuteronomy 8:18)…and the many talents and gifts you now have?

Everyone has friends, but what about those outside your friendly circle? If barriers, borders or any hindrance prevents someone from becoming your friend, or visa-versa, then 'Unity' as God intended is none existent.

The Middle East, as an example, is by far dominantly controlled by the Muslim faith. That particular part of the world has been in constant chaos since man first stepped foot upon the soil. Why? Religion! Christ was not and is not part of 98% of that culture, and apart from Him, 'Unity', in the truest sense of the word, is unable to exist. Good and evil cannot mix anymore than oil and water can; author has Muslim acquaintances and judges no man/woman.

I respect and try to love all people, no matter their faith. What you choose to believe is your business…and you should have the freedom to choose what you believe in without repercussion of any kind, as Christians do…but as for me and my family, we will serve the Lord.

Joshua 24:15 reads…"But if you are unwilling to serve the Lord, then, choose today whom you will serve. Would you prefer the gods your ancestors served beyond the Euphrates? Or will it be the gods of the

Amorites in whose land you now live? But as for me and my family, we will serve the Lord."

And to further answer the question, what more do I need? … Let me ask," If you died today, where are you going?" Or do you care!

I believe you should care. I believe it to be in your best interest to humble and submit your ways to the living, holy and righteous God, learning to live in 'Unity' with all people, than it is to die and spend eternity separated from God, our Creator, the CEO of the universe.

God teaches us four things in Luke 16:19-31.

- There is conscious existence after death!
- The reality and torment of Hell is realized!
- Once you die, there is no second chance!
- It is impossible for the dead to communicate with the living! (16:26)

In other words, we will know we are dead, but unable to do anything about it…Hell will become the reality and place we have always heard and read about…when we realize what has happened, and time for a change of heart will be non-existent…and finally, as much as we would like to come back from the dead to warn our family, friends, etc., about the Hell-hole we have discovered, this will not be possible.

BLACK & WHITE

Living life according to plan

U = Unity---Chapter 3

Behold, how good and how pleasant it is for brethren to dwell together in 'Unity'! Psalm 133:1 (KJV)

Let us choose 'Unity' over envy and jealousy. (KS)

But you're a believer and 'you' have nothing to worry about correct?

You have taken on the 'Yoke' of God, who has become your personal 'Overseer' enabling you to live in 'Unity' with all peoples, until the day He calls you home to spend eternity with Him, isn't that right!

Let me clarify an important point by asking this specific question?
Who is the person in your life that you trust the most, unconditionally, no matter what your circumstances?

If your answer is not Jesus Christ, then you are bound for problems. Our priorities in life are in desperate need of change. We see them as anything but what God intended them to be. God is seldom in the picture. The formula that is missing and the very one we need, is "God, *Self*, Family, & Career," the title of the second book in this series, and a life changing read for all; you're not alone when thinking this is backwards!

In Matthew 10:37-39 (NLT) Jesus says…37 "If you love your father or mother more than you love me, you are not worthy of being mine; or if you love your son or daughter more than me, you are not worthy of being mine. 38 If you refuse to take up your cross and follow me, you are not worthy of being mine. 39 If you cling to your life, you will lose it; but if you give it up for me, you will find it."

U = Unity---Chapter 3

Behold, how good and how pleasant it is for brethren to dwell together in 'Unity'! Psalm 133:1 (KJV)

Let us choose 'Unity' over envy and jealousy. (KS)

In Romans 10:9 Paul tells us, ... "*For if you confess with your mouth that Jesus is Lord and believe in your heart that God raised him from the dead, you will be saved*"... this path is needed to begin experiencing the awesome truth of God and how 'Unity' comes with the package.

We might relate this to putting on the armor of God. More clearly, it means knowing and living out the word of God by way of believing in, and having a personal relationship with His Son, Jesus Christ.

Christ is the Author of Life. Through Him we discover true wisdom and knowledge, leading us to the understanding we need... (Colossians 2:3)...and by way of this channel we are able to fully grasp and exercise the fullness and obligation of true 'Unity'. Amen!

Only when we humble ourselves to the fact that it's not feasible for us to think we (created), are wiser than the one who (Creator), provided all wisdom can we experience the power behind setting our priorities.

Christ says in John 13:16... "*How true it is that a servant is not greater than the master. Nor are messengers more important than the one who sends them,*" ... or as it's phrased in the King James Version, "*neither he that is sent greater than he that sent him.*" It makes no sense that the created can be greater than the Creator; religion therefore be debunked!

U = Unity---Chapter 3

Behold, how good and how pleasant it is for brethren to dwell together in 'Unity'! Psalm 133:1 (KJV)

Let us choose 'Unity' over envy and jealousy. (KS)

Jesus is not claiming to be bigger and better than God, He is God, and really, what makes us think that we can take what we did not create, being wisdom in this case, and be wise in our own eyes?

I can picture the look on my brothers face who owns a small, but very successful custom home business, if I were to say to him, "Rick, the way you are building your homes is all wrong and let me make a few suggestions." Who am I to tell him what he should and should not be doing when I'm unable to draw a straight line with a ruler in my hand?

Majority of critics of the Holy Bible and the Christian faith have never read but a few pages of said book, so how can they be true critics; of any topic if they have never done sufficient research into topic of concern?

On another note, when Jesus was approached and asked the question about whether it was right to pay taxes to the Roman Government or not, He responded by saying in Matthew 22:21... "Give to Caesar what is Caesar's... and to God what is God's."

There is no other explanation, provable on the face of this planet that God, as in the Holy Bible, The Father, The Son and The Holy Spirit, did not speak everything into existence today as we know and see it to be.

U = Unity---Chapter 3

Behold, how good and how pleasant it is for brethren to dwell together in 'Unity'! Psalm 133:1 (KJV)

Let us choose 'Unity' over envy and jealousy. (KS)

Therefore, only when we accept absolute truth in Christ by faith, can we begin to celebrate true 'Unity' with all persons, no matter their critique, beliefs or opinion of Christians. And just as importantly, in order to have answers beyond human understanding placed upon our lips to share with others in and for 'Unity', Christ needs to be our number one focal point, meaning, being in the driver's seat of our lives.

Have you ever felt hatred toward another or perhaps experienced the effects of it? What about jealousy or envy? How about covetousness?

Have you ever had one too many drinks, finding yourself out of sorts and speaking out of turn, about yourself or matters of confidentiality?

Have you ever felt the veins in your head swell from shouts of anger? I have! I cannot and will not lie. Considering that 'folly' has been around since the fall of man, I too have had my share of giving and receiving this 'folly' and it's not something I am proud of. I've hated and been hated! I've been both jealous and envious! I'm guilty of wishing for what was not mine to be mine! I've been so intoxicated I didn't know which way was up or down. I've been so full of frustration and anger I could literally feel the veins throughout my head bulging, when I was supposed to be setting the example as the only Christian within my own household.

U = Unity---Chapter 3

Behold, how good and how pleasant it is for brethren to dwell together in 'Unity'! Psalm 133:1 (KJV)

Let us choose 'Unity' over envy and jealousy. (KS)

My friend, God never changes, nor have, or will His ways and rules. The created man is the one who changes, not Christ our rock. That's why it's noted as 'Ten Commandments' and not 'Ten Suggestions'.

The evil that is born and rests within man from conception is the foundation of all 'folly' that exists today. **Guns are not the sin problem**...the man that pulls the trigger is the sin problem. **Money is not the sin problem**...the love of money is the sin problem. **Disagreements between man is not the sin problem**...things like selfish ambition, pride or racism is the sin problem.

God directs James to share in James 3:13-16... 13 "If you are wise and understand God's ways, live a life of steady goodness so that only good deeds will pour forth. And if you don't brag about the good you do, then you will be truly wise! 14 But if you are bitterly jealous and there is selfish ambition in your hearts, don't brag about being wise. That is the worst kind of lie. 15 For jealousy and selfishness are not God's kind of wisdom. Such things are earthly, unspiritual, and motivated by the Devil. 16 For wherever there is jealousy and selfish ambition, there you will find disorder and every kind of evil."

Again, we cannot experience complete 'Unity' apart from God. All relationships need to be in harmony with His way of thinking.

BLACK & WHITE

Living life according to plan

U = Unity---Chapter 3

Behold, how good and how pleasant it is for brethren to dwell together in 'Unity'! Psalm 133:1 (KJV)

Let us choose 'Unity' over envy and jealousy. (KS)

Let's say a person were to cut you off while driving and almost put you in the ditch. You could catch them and offer them a piece of your mind! You could promote 'Unity,' being God's preference, and let the incident slide, or one better, if the opportunity presented itself, you could offer a listening ear to the distracted soul that almost put you in the ditch!

Our darker side is as plain as the nose on our face. No one is without sin. As Paul shares in Romans 3:9-10 … 9 Well then, are we Jews better than others? No, not at all, for we have already shown that all people, whether Jews or Gentiles, are under the power of sin. 10 As the Scriptures say (Psalm 14), "No one is good—not even one."

In James 4:1-8, God inspires James in saying…1 "What is causing the quarrels and fights among you? Isn't it the whole army of evil desires at war within you? 2 You want what you don't have, so you scheme and kill to get it. You are jealous for what others have, and you can't possess it, so you fight and quarrel to take it away from them. And yet the reason you don't have what you want is that you don't ask God for it. 3 And even when you do ask, you don't get it because your whole motive is wrong—you want only what will give you pleasure. 4 You adulterers! Don't you realize that friendship with this world makes you an enemy of God? I say it again, that if your aim is to enjoy this world, you can't be a friend of God.

BLACK & WHITE

Living life according to plan

U = Unity---Chapter 3

Behold, how good and how pleasant it is for brethren to dwell together in 'Unity'! Psalm 133:1 (KJV)

Let us choose 'Unity' over envy and jealousy. (KS)

5 What do you think the Scriptures mean when they say that the Holy
Spirit, whom God has placed within us, jealously longs for us to be
faithful? 6 He gives us more and more strength to stand against such evil
desires. As the Scriptures say, "God sets himself against the proud, but
he shows favor to the humble." 7 So humble yourselves before God.
Resist the Devil, and he will flee from you. 8 Draw close to God and
God will draw close to you."

If we would only humble ourselves to recognize the dark side within us, we could be on our way to peace and 'Unity' in the Middle East and throughout the world…to equality and 'Unity' over racism…to truth and 'Unity' within the church, to peace and harmony over denominational differences…including 'Unity' between church, state and public issues of concern without the biased effect.

Ok so I'm appearing somewhat unrealistic.

But I'm thinking, what's so unrealistic about standing firm on morals and values? All we hear today is "you're too conservative" when the conversation is centered around 'absolute truth' or 'right and wrong'. True Christian faith stands void of judgment; it is our true cornerstone.

I am not fearful in proclaiming to a failing world that it needs to change its ways and suggesting '*THE*' means of fixing it.

U = Unity---Chapter 3

Behold, how good and how pleasant it is for brethren to dwell together in 'Unity'! Psalm 133:1 (KJV)

Let us choose 'Unity' over envy and jealousy. (KS)

Why individuals choose to continue living in anger, or denial, in selfishness, cheating, or being deceptive, when the answer is available to them, is hard to grasp. There is a clear cut starting point when God's goodness teaches, 'do unto others, as you would have them do unto you' … while the world continues to favor "do unto others before they do unto you"?

The more I get thinking about it, if I were to be labeled as anything during my brief life span, then let it be as one fearless and unashamed of the Gospel, proclaiming it to be the solution for 'all' societal problems.

If someone chooses to continue living with a correctable issue in their life, deliberately ignoring the help around them, are they not then choosing to remain part of the problem rather than part of the solution? God's intention was to have men everywhere living in 'Unity'. How is this possible if man will not admit and correct his own weaknesses?

I believe Solomon addressed this as the folly of man.

The word 'FOL'LY' in Webster's 1828 Dictionary is described as:

Weakness of intellect; imbecility of mind; want of understanding; 'A fool layeth open his folly,' Proverbs 13:16.

U = Unity---Chapter 3

Behold, how good and how pleasant it is for brethren to dwell together in 'Unity'! Psalm 133:1 (KJV)

Let us choose 'Unity' over envy and jealousy. (KS)

A weak or absurd act not highly criminal; an act, which is inconsistent with the dictates of reason, or with the ordinary rules of prudence. In this sense it may be used in the singular, but is generally in the plural. Hence we speak of the follies of youth.

An absurd act, which is highly sinful; any conduct contrary to the laws of God or man; sin; scandalous crimes; that which violates moral precepts and dishonors the offender. Shechem wrought folly in Israel. Achan wrought folly in Israel. Gen. 34. Josh. 7.

Criminal weakness; depravity of mind

Proverbs 5:22-23 says… 22 "An evil man is held captive by his own sins; they are ropes that catch and hold him." 23 "He will die for lack of self-control; he will be lost because of his incredible folly."

It is often said that he who commits 'FOL'LY' is unwise or a 'FOOL'.

The word 'FOOL' in Webster's 1828 Dictionary is described as…

…One who is destitute of reason, or the common powers of understanding.

BLACK & WHITE

Living life according to plan

U = Unity---Chapter 3

Behold, how good and how pleasant it is for brethren to dwell together in 'Unity'! Psalm 133:1 (KJV)

Let us choose 'Unity' over envy and jealousy. (KS)

…In common language, a person who is somewhat deficient in intellect, but not an idiot; or a person who acts absurdly; one who does not exercise his reason; one who pursues a course contrary to the dictates of wisdom.

…In scripture, fool is often used for a wicked or depraved person; one who acts contrary to sound wisdom in his moral deportment; one who follows his own inclinations, who prefers trifling and temporary pleasures to the service of God and eternal happiness.

…A weak Christian; a godly person who has much remaining sin and unbelief.

In Ps. 14 we read… "The fool hath said in his heart, there is no God."

In Luke 24 we read… "O fools, and slow of heart to believe all the prophets have written."

So there you have it my friend!

God is as ideal and absolute as it comes, and just as Psalm 133:1 says, "How good and pleasant it is for brethren to dwell together in 'Unity'."

BLACK & WHITE

Living life according to plan

U = Unity---Chapter 3

Behold, how good and how pleasant it is for brethren to dwell together in 'Unity'! Psalm 133:1 (KJV)

Let us choose 'Unity' over envy and jealousy. (KS)

Yes, I am speaking to you throughout this book instituting my own bias, regarding the fact that it be in our best interest to 'Yoke' ourselves with God and learn His ways…allowing Him to be our 'Overseer' for life, and from His love and guidance we learn to live as He intended…in 'Unity', apart from envy, jealousy and the likes of the corrupted, foul and foolish minds who choose to stay the course of deliberate sin, while ignoring the gift of change and betterment; not to mention for our own best sake.

The need to live in 'Unity', at peace, in humbleness and tolerance with all God's children saved or unsaved is essential and a process that takes time. It becomes second nature for those who have accepted and allowed themselves to genuinely mature in the truth and Spirit of His word. As Paul has said in 2 Timothy 4:7… "*I have fought the good fight, I have finished the race, I have kept the faith.*"

YOU ARE WORTH IT and deserve to live in a world where God intended for all Brethren to dwell in 'Unity'. Make the most of the 'Yoke' of God…and learn the benefits of walking in the integrity and wisdom of Jesus Christ and not that of a carnal and dark world.

Amen to Unity!

A = Abstain---Chapter 4

Prove all things; hold fast that which is good. 'Abstain' from all appearance of evil. 1 Thessalonians 5:21-22 (KJV)
Let us 'Abstain' from all that is not of God. (KS)

Webster's 1828 dictionary describes 'Abstain' as follows:

[In a general sense, 'Abstain' means to forbear, or refrain from, voluntarily; but used chiefly to denote a restraint upon the passions or appetites; to refrain from indulgence.]

The bible teaches us to 'Abstain' from all appearance of evil and if we are to boast we are to boast in the Lord…and that is why I am here. That is why this book is in your hands right now…why I am a stronger and wiser person today, not by self or by works but by faith in Jesus Christ. Through Him, lies the ability to 'Abstain' from the sinful indulgence of our lustful passions and appetites that are plaguing our homes, schools, government offices, churches and legal systems today and escalating in quantum leaps.

Apart from Christ, we are haunted by what is known as the sinful nature. Everyone born today is born into sin and needs to place their faith and trust in Jesus Christ who died on the cross as the perfect sacrifice, the unblemished Lamb of God, spilling His blood as a final atonement for all our sins.
Leviticus 17:11 says," *It is the blood, representing life, that brings you atonement.*" Meaning, through Christ, defeating death when God raised Him from the dead is the new life, as in 'born again' that all us sinners need and must accept prior to our last breath; when will you take yours?

BLACK & WHITE

Living life according to plan

A = Abstain---Chapter 4

Prove all things; hold fast that which is good. 'Abstain' from all appearance of evil. 1 Thessalonians 5:21-22 (KJV)

Let us 'Abstain' from all that is not of God. (KS)

You will recall back on page '11' where I said; While the world is built on hatred, jealousy, gossip, selfish ambition, greed and violence...God builds on, "love, joy, peace, patience, kindness, goodness, faithfulness, gentleness and self-control!"

These comparisons can be found in the book of Galatians 5:19-23...and I want to take a moment to share with you a bit of Paul's words from the book of Romans 8:1-6, to more clearly compare our sinful nature to that of the spiritual nature that comes upon us as a result of putting our faith and trust in Jesus Christ.

Paul says this: 1 "So now there is no condemnation for those who belong to Christ Jesus. 2 For the power of the life-giving Spirit has freed you through Christ Jesus from the power of sin that leads to death. 3 The Law of Moses could not save us, because of our sinful nature. But God put into effect a different plan to save us. He sent his own Son in a human body like ours, except that ours are sinful. God destroyed sin's control over us by giving his Son as a sacrifice for our sins. 4 He did this so that the requirement of the law would be fully accomplished for us who no longer follow our sinful nature but instead follow the Spirit. 5 Those who are dominated by the sinful nature think about sinful things, but those who are controlled by the Holy Spirit think about things that please the Spirit. 6 If your sinful nature controls your mind, there is death. But if the Holy Spirit controls your mind, there is life and peace". *Verse 6 alone is huge for any one, any soul*!

A = Abstain---Chapter 4

Prove all things; hold fast that which is good. 'Abstain' from all appearance of evil. 1 Thessalonians 5:21-22 (KJV)
Let us 'Abstain' from all that is not of God. (KS)

For me, the word 'sinner' which I may have heard a half dozen times in my first twenty-nine years of life, somehow sounded corny or weird, so I never paid it any attention. No one ever said to me, "Kevin, you're a sinner and you need to put your trust in Jesus Christ!" Sad but true.

If I recall correctly, whenever I heard the word 'sin' mentioned, it was in passing, thrown out as a joke or a dig rather than from someone who was actually referring to the need to repent of our sins.

We need to 'Abstain' from all unrighteousness, as the result, otherwise it leads to death, including permanent separation from His wonderful and marvelous grace for eternity; this is not a wishy-washy matter!

Yes I believe in, 'once saved always saved' unless we rebuke/deny the Holy Spirit. Not everyone sees it that way and that's fine. Christ Himself said in Mark 9:40--- "Anyone who is not against us is for us".

Please do not misunderstand this to include the cults or liberal Christianity, both renowned for dissecting scripture to entertain thirsty and/or financially supportive ears. John says in 2 John 1:10-11... "If anyone comes to you and does not bring this teaching, do not take him into your house or welcome him. Anyone who welcomes him shares in his wicked work."

BLACK & WHITE

Living life according to plan

A = Abstain---Chapter 4

Prove all things; hold fast that which is good. 'Abstain' from all appearance of evil. 1 Thessalonians 5:21-22 (KJV)

Let us 'Abstain' from all that is not of God. (KS)

I also believe 'rebuke' to be healthy and necessary as well in assisting us to 'Abstain' from the overwhelming temptations of our day, and in keeping us accountable to the word.

We then need to bring this rebuke before God for clarification. Is it He who is using this person to keep us or put us back on track? If we are out of line scripturally then we need to be corrected.

God shows no favoritism…He directs Paul in Colossians 3:25 (NIV) by saying… "Anyone who does wrong will be repaid for his wrong, and there is no favoritism." Also, God uses Solomon in Proverbs 9:9 (KJV) by saying… "Give instruction to a wise man, and he will be yet wiser." Meaning, a man led of God should always be open to constructive rebuke from other fellow Christians, and then verify in God's word for confirmation and clarification.

The most remarkable thing for me since accepting Christ as my 'Overseer' is that I was not as willing to humble myself to listening and learning as I am today. When I first read James 1:19-20, 19 "My dear brothers and sisters, be quick to listen, slow to speak, and slow to get angry" and then tied it in with the wisdom of Solomon for example in Proverbs 29:20--- "Do you see a man who speaks in haste? There is more hope for a fool than for him"…I suddenly realized the **gigantic gap that was in deep need of repair within me**.

BLACK & WHITE

Living life according to plan

A = Abstain---Chapter 4

Prove all things; hold fast that which is good. 'Abstain' from all appearance of evil. 1 Thessalonians 5:21-22 (KJV)
Let us 'Abstain' from all that is not of God. (KS)

We need to…prove all things: hold fast that which is good and 'Abstain' from all appearance of evil.

2 Corinthians 11:14 says… "Even Satan can disguise himself as an angel of light." (Anything appearing to be good, but is not)

Therefore, as we continue to accept just anything that comes our way, without testing it against God's word, then we leave ourselves vulnerable to the seduction of every kind of evil attack--- "The sinful nature wants to do evil, which is just the opposite of what the Spirit wants. And the Spirit gives us desires that are the opposite of what the sinful nature desires. These two forces are constantly fighting each other, so you are not free to carry out your good intentions."…Galatians 5:17

Satan is at work 24/7, 365 days a year deceiving our minds into believing that there are no consequences for our sin. **Big time wrong**!

Again I make reference to an earlier comment that reads… The purpose of this book is to inspire, motivate and encourage you to consider 'Godly' change--- To walk in true integrity as did Jesus Christ --- Living and breathing the **inerrant, infallible word of God**, Genesis to Revelation, *never claiming perfection* but mastering our weaknesses.

BLACK & WHITE

Living life according to plan

A = Abstain---Chapter 4

Prove all things; hold fast that which is good. 'Abstain' from all appearance of evil. 1 Thessalonians 5:21-22 (KJV)
Let us 'Abstain' from all that is not of God. (KS)

We cannot become this kind of people, as long as we continue denying the power of the sinful nature within us…the very nature that satan is determined to keep using to rule our lives.

The strength we need to 'Abstain' from the unrighteousness of this world is called grace. The grace of God provides us a humble and righteous spirit that begins to work on the troubled areas of our lives.

As an example, I can say without reservation that I went into marriage blindfolded. I was there for all the wrong reasons. The lusts and pleasures of this world drew me into marriage…meaning; I was seduced by way of worldly deception and not by God's leading…therefore, I could not deny the sinful nature within me that can only be corrected by the grace of God. I could have prevented much, but chose to do nothing, out of ignorance. I was focused on the temporal and not the eternal, which is God.

I only came to trust Christ when my second marriage failed. However, I quickly settled back into my old ways…never seeking out a church, Christian friends, or more importantly, I never read the Bible, about the 'One' who said He could save me and teach me if I was willing to listen and learn. And what does God teach us about the humble?

BLACK & WHITE

Living life according to plan

A = Abstain---Chapter 4

Prove all things; hold fast that which is good. 'Abstain' from all appearance of evil. 1 Thessalonians 5:21-22 (KJV)

Let us 'Abstain' from all that is not of God. (KS)

Meanwhile, in the midst of my old sinful nature, I met my third wife, and two years into that marriage, it also began to fall apart. But by the grace of God we recently celebrated our 25th wedding anniversary. God clearly showed me how I could continue doing things my way, being unhappy and unfulfilled, or, start learning from Him and live with contentment and joy; not without issue and struggle, but with peace. He wasn't lying…And how pathetic to think of all the lives I hurt out of ignorance through two previous marriages/families, and up until the very day I came to trust in Him and Him alone; totally unnecessary.

But as Christians, **does fun not disappear as boredom sets in**?

Not all actions are evil…nor are all things fun and pleasurable, taboo, because we are Christians…The Christian life *can be* (a book on its own merit), anything but boring.

As an example, a couple shared with me that after becoming Christians the one spouse still favored a local casino for fun…where the other immediately recognized the unwise choices they had been making. Although they experienced a little havoc in the beginning, they soon discovered that what they were gambling away at a local casino and/or spending on a few other unwise choices, they could actually save, spending the occasional one or two evenings away, building quality memorable moments as a couple, which prior to this they were not

A = Abstain---Chapter 4

Prove all things; hold fast that which is good. 'Abstain' from all appearance of evil. 1 Thessalonians 5:21-22 (KJV)
Let us 'Abstain' from all that is not of God. (KS)

doing. Plus they could be giving more to the needs of our world locally and abroad. **As a side note**, this one spouse and her mother averaged $400 p/m each, and over 10 years, had jointly donated $100K to casino.

Proverbs 13:20 says… "Whoever walks with the wise will become wise; whoever walks with fools will suffer harm."

Proverbs 17:16 teaches… "It is senseless to pay tuition to educate a fool, since he has no heart for learning."

The idea here is that the company we keep will influence the decisions we make, especially when it concerns money.

In finishing off this chapter, let me leave you with a few thoughts…

- What if we were to change today, to 'Abstain' from all unrighteousness, in favour of building a legacy of profound integrity?

- What if we were to live with honor, making honourable decisions, even in the midst of temptation to justify less than honourable behaviour?

- What if we were to be honest at all times, in all matters, even when it hurt us to do so?

BLACK & WHITE

Living life according to plan

A = Abstain---Chapter 4

Prove all things; hold fast that which is good. 'Abstain' from all appearance of evil. 1 Thessalonians 5:21-22 (KJV)

Let us 'Abstain' from all that is not of God. (KS)

- What if we were to take personal and business responsibility for all our actions and mistakes, without looking to family, friends, government, schools or other authorities to justify or blame our wrong decisions?

- What if we were to commit to the purity of love, saving our bodies and hearts for the one we will marry?

- What if we were to commit to the morals and tradition of family and marriage, a mother and a father, and treasured our word as our bond at the altar?

- What if we were to seek our life purpose from our Creator and lived to fulfill that purpose?

- And what if we were to stand firm, living under the absolute, provable truth and authority of Jesus Christ?

WHAT IF WE, TODAY, CHOSE TO ABSTAIN FROM ALL UNRIGHTEOUSNESS AND FINISH OFF OUR DAYS IN THIS WAY?

I'M IN!

R = Repent---Chapter 5

Be zealous therefore, and 'repent'. Revelation 3:19 (KJV)
To 'Repent' is to have regret of our sins and willingly choose to ask God in Jesus' name for His forgiveness (KS)

Webster's 1828 dictionary explains 'Repent' as follows:

...To feel pain, sorrow or regret for something done or spoken; as, to repent that we have lost much time in idleness or sensual pleasure; to repent that we have injured or wounded the feelings of a friend. A person repents only of what he himself has done or said.

...To change the mind in consequence of the inconvenience or injury done by past conduct.

...Applied to the Supreme Being, to change the course of providential dealings. Genesis 6. Psalm 106.

...In theology, to sorrow or be pained for sin, as a violation of God's holy law, a dishonor to His character and government, and the foulest ingratitude to a being of infinite benevolence.

Except ye repent, ye shall all likewise perish. Luke 13. Acts 3.

He does not want anyone to perish, so he is giving more time for everyone to repent. 2 Peter 3:9

R = Repent---Chapter 5

Be zealous therefore, and 'repent'. Revelation 3:19 (KJV)
To 'Repent' is to have regret of our sins and willingly choose to ask God in Jesus' name for His forgiveness (KS)

Thus far we've taken on the 'Yoke' of God to learn His ways, chosen Him to be our 'Overseer', enabling true love to live in 'Unity' with all people, learning how and why we need to 'Abstain' from all temptations of evil…and then growing to a level of maturity in understanding and appreciation for our need to 'Repent' of all our wrong doings. When we do so God forgives us our sins, cancelling immediately, as though they never were, expecting us to learn from error and to sin no more.

The world has endorsed SOR'RY in place of 'Repent'.

Webster's says of SOR'RY… [Grieved for the loss of some good; pained for some evil that has happened to one's self or friends or country. It does not ordinarily imply severe grief, but rather slight or transient regret. It may be however, and often is used to express deep grief. We are sorry to lose the company of those we love; we are sorry to lose friends or property; we are sorry for the misfortunes of our friends or of our country.]

Saying we are SOR'RY for a wrong, in actuality, is nothing more than a simple and/or temporary brush-off…void of the 'POWER' (of the Holy Spirit) to genuinely change the heart. As noted above, SOR'RY implies slight or transient regret. When it comes to God, He deserves and expects only the sincerest of hearts in regards to repentance, and only through His grace and gift of the Holy Spirit can true repentance be accomplished.

R = Repent---Chapter 5

Be zealous therefore, and 'repent'. Revelation 3:19 (KJV)
To 'Repent' is to have regret of our sins and willingly choose to ask God in Jesus' name for His forgiveness (KS)

The word, 'UNFEIGNEDLY' an adverb meaning, (without hypocrisy; really; sincerely) is more in line with what God expects. And since He created us, knowing intimately our sinful hearts' desire, He knows whether we mean SOR'RY or are eternally sincere about our need to 'Repent' of all sin without the slightest hint of hypocrisy.[He pardoneth all them that truly 'Repent', and unfeignedly believe his holy gospel.]

Are you grasping the power behind this simple act of faith?

All we need do, with a sincere and repentant heart, is say, "*Lord, I am a sinner, and I repent of all my sins, every wrong thought or deed in my life... please forgive me and help me to seek and accomplish your will and passion for my life. Thank you for creating all that exists, especially your Son, Jesus Christ, whom you sent to die on the cross for my sins and the sins of every individual on your magnificent universe...Thank you for having your Son defeat death, by raising Him from the dead on the third day just as You promised...Here and now, I accept and invite you, dear Jesus, to come into my heart as my personal Lord and Savior...lead me and guide me and fill me with your Holy Spirit, that I might become everything you intended for me, all for your glory... Amen*!"

R = Repent---Chapter 5

Be zealous therefore, and 'repent'. Revelation 3:19 (KJV)

To 'Repent' is to have regret of our sins and willingly choose to ask God in Jesus' name for His forgiveness (KS)

If you unfeignedly repeated the above statement, believing wholeheartedly in Romans 10:9, "*For if you confess with your mouth that Jesus is Lord and believe in your heart that God raised him from the dead, you will be saved*" then, you have accomplished much by faith without the need for works. In actual fact, you have repented of your sins, asking for forgiveness, and God has forgiven and wiped out forever, every sin you have ever committed since birth as though they never were. Now that's grace!

If you had of asked God to list all your sins, seconds before your act of repentance, He could have easily done so. But the instant you confessed those sins, asking Him to forgive you, He fulfilled His promise by voiding them instantaneously. To ask God about those sins following repentance, He would only reply "What sins?" for He is a holy and righteous God who does not lie, and tells us in Psalm 89:35 (Aramaic bible), "*Once I have sworn in my holiness to David and I shall not lie*."

So most importantly, celebrate that your name is now written in the book of life (See Luke 10:20). You have stepped from death, into life eternal by the power and grace of God…the Creator of all things. He sent His Son, Jesus Christ incarnate, to die on the cross for our sins, making available eternal life for anyone who asks and believes. (See John 3:16)

We can 'Repent' and live forever. It really is that simple!

BLACK & WHITE

Living life according to plan

R = Repent---Chapter 5

Be zealous therefore, and 'repent'. Revelation 3:19 (KJV)

To 'Repent' is to have regret of our sins and willingly choose to ask God in Jesus' name for His forgiveness (KS)

We recall the fall of Television Evangelist, Reverend Jimmy Swaggart and the promiscuous escapades of a past President of the United States, Bill Clinton!

I'm using these two examples as they depict a similar case of temptation that got the better of two powerful and prominent individuals, but non-the less, each succumbed to sin, both are human, created, not Creator!

No matter who we are, a man or woman of God, a President of The United States, a celebrity, or a happily married individual, we are all human and susceptible to temptation and acts of sin whether we like it or will admit it or not. "We all fall short of God's glorious standard" (Romans 3:23).

Now, I'm being totally unbiased in this brief comparison as I point out what I believe to be a clear indication of the difference between repentance and merely saying, "I'm SOR'RY" at the least.

On international and world television the world witnessed both these individuals, Reverend Jimmy Swaggart, and President Bill Clinton, being handed an opportunity to repent of their sins before God and the viewers. One man repented and apologized, and the other did nothing but deny his guilt. To this day, the one who did nothing but deny his guilt is exalted while the other, despised by both world and Christian.

R = Repent---Chapter 5

Be zealous therefore, and 'repent'. Revelation 3:19 (KJV)
To 'Repent' is to have regret of our sins and willingly choose to ask God in Jesus' name for His forgiveness (KS)

Clearly, before God and all the listening and viewing audience of international and world television, Reverend Jimmy Swaggart apologized, wept, and asked God and the world to forgive him, for the sin he had committed. In actual fact, Reverend Swaggart went beyond saying he was SOR'RY, by choosing to 'Repent' of his sinful actions.

It was quite evident to anyone appreciating the act of true repentance that Reverend Swaggart did indeed 'Repent', and did so unfeignedly. And I believe in that instant, God wiped away his act of sin and bestowed forgiveness, encouraging, GO AND SIN NO MORE! Rev. Jimmy Swaggart was a man who had the courage and humbleness, available only by the grace of God, to confess, do and say what needed to be done, in all humility, to be rid of the vileness that eats away our souls until repentance is real and true, thanks be to God.

Where would we be without the grace of God allowing us to 'Repent'? We would be exactly where we are today. Look around us! Read the front page of the newspaper. Listen to the radio. We are where we are today because we refuse to know God the way He desires us to know Him…without prejudice, bias, or idols. God says in Exodus 20:5, "*I, the Lord your God, am a jealous God. I do not leave unpunished, the sins of those who hate me.*"

We believe or we don't. We are hot or cold; for God or against Him.

R = Repent---Chapter 5

Be zealous therefore, and 'repent'. Revelation 3:19 (KJV)

To 'Repent' is to have regret of our sins and willingly choose to ask God in Jesus' name for His forgiveness (KS)

Likewise, and clearly before God and all the listening and viewing audience of international and world television, former President Bill Clinton did not apologize, nor did he say he was SOR'RY for his wrongful misconduct until months later; again **sorry is not to repent**! As a matter of fact, his response when initially asked if said accusations against him were true, was 'no'.

*** *President Clinton left the impression, not just to the people of the United States, but to the world watching, especially our children, that lying, money, power and position can take precedence over integrity, honesty and truth.*

Rather than admitting his error in judgment and confessing that the allegations were true, he allowed his pride to take over, only to be proven by fact, he was both a liar and a fool. Proverbs 16:5, 16:18 reads as follows: **5** The Lord despises pride; be assured that the proud will be punished. **18** Pride goes before destruction and haughtiness before a fall.

Even in his book, 'My Life', it's been clarified once again by his former mistress, Monica Lewinsky, that it too is full of lies. If I may be so blunt in sharing another wise tidbit for us all to learn by, Proverbs 26:11 says, "As a dog returns to its vomit, so a fool repeats his foolishness.."

R = Repent---Chapter 5

Be zealous therefore, and 'repent'. Revelation 3:19 (KJV)
To 'Repent' is to have regret of our sins and willingly choose to ask God in Jesus' name for His forgiveness (KS)

Everyone is capable of error. That is sin. No one is exempt from taking bad turns. And no mistake is beyond repair when God is part of the picture. Without Him we discover our burdens are too heavy and we quit. We give up on ourselves, our families, and our work, and all close to us.

Not knowing God, we attempt to fill the void with alcohol, drugs, affairs, extended work hours, and the uncontrollable compulsion for money and the sorts. In Matthew 11:28, Jesus says to us, "Come to me, all of you who are weary and carry heavy burdens, and I will give you rest."

There is nothing wrong with admitting our weaknesses. Everyone has them! To truly 'Repent' takes courage I'll admit, but it also takes us to a whole new level of understanding and appreciation of ourselves. Also, Proverbs 28:13 says, "*People who conceal their sins will not prosper, but if they confess and turn from them, they will receive mercy*."

The Holy Bible is the most ridiculed, argued and protested book on our planet, and in addition, God is the only author who is and remains actively involved in a reader's life by the Power of The Holy Spirit.

'Repent' my friend. Trust God. Start with the sinner's prayer at the bottom of page 77. Ground yourself in a Bible believing and teaching Church. Surround yourself with Christian friends and get wisdom.

E = Edify---Chapter 6

Therefore comfort each other and 'Edify' one another, just as you also are doing. 1 Thessalonians 5:11 (NKJV)

Let us always 'Edify' one another in the wisdom, knowledge and understanding of our Creator. (KS)

Webster's 1828 dictionary says to 'Edify' is to instruct and improve the mind in knowledge generally, and particularly in moral and religious knowledge, in faith and holiness.

An idea I like from author Stephen Covey, renowned for the book, 'The 7 Habits of Highly Effective People' is that he suggests the best way for us to retain and learn new information is to immediately begin teaching others what we have learned; brilliant!

Jesus said to us in Matthew 28:19-20, "Therefore, go and make disciples of all the nations, baptizing them in the name of the Father and the Son and the Holy Spirit. Teach these new disciples to obey all the commands I have given you."

In other words…we are not to keep the good news to ourselves. We are to go and teach to others what we have learned. Teach them about me, to live for me and with me… for I am God, your solitude, your refuge and hope in times of need and turmoil.

We are privileged to 'Edify' one another, to instruct and improve the mind in moral and religious knowledge, as well as in faith and holiness of our Lord and Savior Jesus Christ. It's an enjoyable, yet challenging commission, but worthy for even the sake of one lost soul.

BLACK & WHITE

Living life according to plan

E = Edify---Chapter 6

Therefore comfort each other and 'Edify' one another, just as you also are doing. 1 Thessalonians 5:11 (NKJV)

Let us always 'Edify' one another in the wisdom, knowledge and understanding of our Creator. (KS)

Jesus says in Luke 15:10; "There is rejoicing in the presence of the Angels of God over one sinner who repents."

We knew nothing of knowledge, until Genesis 2:9…after which time God had finished creating the heavens and the earth in their entire vast array, 6 days worth, and adding the 7th day as a day of rest. "*And the Lord God planted all sorts of trees in the garden—beautiful trees that produced delicious fruit. At the center of the garden he placed the tree of life and the tree of the knowledge of good and evil.*"

We then read in Genesis 2:15-17, 15 "The Lord God placed the man in the Garden of Eden to tend and care for it." 16 But the Lord God gave him this warning: "You may freely eat any fruit in the garden 17 except fruit from the tree of the knowledge of good and evil. If you eat of its fruit, you will surely die."

So for us to 'Edify' one another, we need first to appreciate that God's intention was solely for man to have a natural 'understanding' within the existence of life as He created it, void of any evil. A wholesome, uncomplicated understanding…how to survive, how to share, how to laugh, how to have fellowship, how to worship, how to give thanks, how to reproduce---and all without shame, need or hard labor.

BLACK & WHITE

Living life according to plan

E = Edify---Chapter 6

Therefore comfort each other and 'Edify' one another, just as you also are doing. 1 Thessalonians 5:11 (NKJV)

Let us always 'Edify' one another in the wisdom, knowledge and understanding of our Creator. (KS)

But that all changed in Genesis 3:6-7 where we read:

6 The woman was convinced. The fruit looked so fresh and delicious, and it would make her so wise. So she ate some of the fruit. (She was deceived) She also gave some to her husband, who was with her. Then he ate it, too. (He also was deceived… Death and eternal separation from God became reality). 7 At that moment, their eyes were opened, and they suddenly felt shame at their nakedness.

In an instant, when Eve ate of the fruit, and then did Adam, from the tree of the knowledge of good and evil, which they were sternly warned not to do, the simple, uncomplicated understanding, that we were blessed with for eternity, was replaced with a complex eternal struggle between two powers known as good and evil; God, and without God!

Life changed immediately and permanently for man and woman...and the entire future of the human race.

First, the uncomplicated and painless childbearing was replaced with intense pain and suffering during childbirth (Genesis 3:16).

Secondly, her husband went from being co-existent with her to headship over her. (Genesis 3:16) [**not meant as superiority**!]

BLACK & WHITE

Living life according to plan

E = Edify---Chapter 6

Therefore comfort each other and 'Edify' one another, just as you also are doing. 1 Thessalonians 5:11 (NKJV)

Let us always 'Edify' one another in the wisdom, knowledge and understanding of our Creator. (KS)

Life also changed immediately and permanently for the man.

First, the ease of plentiful food and having it provided was replaced with a cursed ground and by painful toil he would eat of it all the days of his life. (Genesis 3:17)

Secondly, the once fertile soil will now produce thorns and thistles and by the sweat of his brow, he will eat of the plants of the field (***Created vegetarians Genesis 3:18 - Carnivores Genesis 9:3***) until he returns to the dust from which he came (Genesis 3:18-19). Eternal freedom was replaced with eternal bondage.

When they could have lived forever, without toil, sweat, pain, or suffering, they chose disobedience under the evil and sly deception of satan himself, disguised as a serpent…to which God said in Genesis 3:14-15…"*Because you have done this, you will be punished. You are singled out from all the domestic and wild animals of the whole earth to be cursed. You will grovel in the dust as long as you live, crawling along on your belly. From now on, you and the woman will be enemies, and your offspring and her offspring will be enemies. He will crush your head, and you will strike his heel.*"

In an instant we lost life and inherited death. Today, by the grace of God, through Christ (the bridge), we can win back life and defeat death.

BLACK & WHITE

Living life according to plan

E = Edify---Chapter 6

Therefore comfort each other and 'Edify' one another, just as you also are doing. 1 Thessalonians 5:11 (NKJV)

Let us always 'Edify' one another in the wisdom, knowledge and understanding of our Creator. (KS)

Please allow me to shed some light on the last line of **Genesis 3:15**, the **bible's first recorded prophecy** that says, "He will crush your head, and you will strike his heel."

God is speaking of His Son Jesus Christ, the coming Messiah. That is why He says, "He will crush your head" and "you (satan) will strike His heel", because He, the Christ, will be, (is) the woman's offspring, the One to crush satan's head as He defeats death on the cross, rising from the dead on the third day as promised in His word.

God relayed the bible's first prophecy to satan Himself and personally saw to its fulfillment in the New Testament with the resurrection of Christ, His Son, as He raised Him from the dead, on the third day, fulfilling the promises of scripture. (See Matthew 16:21 and then 1 Corinthians 15:4)

The prophecies recorded in Scripture, when fulfilled, afford most convincing evidence of the divine origin of the Scriptures, as those who uttered the prophecies could not have foreknown the events predicted without supernatural instruction (2 Peter 1:12-21).

'Gospel' means 'good news' correct; so let's check out some further good news!

BLACK & WHITE

Living life according to plan

E = Edify---Chapter 6

Therefore comfort each other and 'Edify' one another, just as you also are doing. 1 Thessalonians 5:11 (NKJV)

Let us always 'Edify' one another in the wisdom, knowledge and understanding of our Creator. (KS)

Let's read what Paul says in Romans 5:17-19. (See Romans 5:12-21)
17 "The sin of this one man, Adam, caused death to rule over us, but all
who receive God's wonderful, gracious gift of righteousness will live in
triumph over sin and death through this one man, Jesus Christ. 18 Yes,
Adam's one sin brought condemnation upon everyone, but Christ's one
act of righteousness makes all people right in God's sight and gives them
life. 19 Because one person disobeyed God, many people became
sinners. But because one other person obeyed God, many people will be
made right in God's sight."

You will recall from earlier on where I mentioned that death and eternal separation from God became a reality the moment Adam ate of the fruit! Well now, because of Christ's one act of righteousness, as prophesied by God to the serpent (satan), that his head would be crushed…this is that **prophecy being fulfilled**.

Christ is that seed of the woman, and He crushes the head of the serpent, as He is raised from the dead, defeating death, which was brought on by satan through the deception of Eve and Adam, causing eternal separation from God.

Today, the way is clear for us through the blood of Christ on the cross, through His death and His resurrection, that we be restored once again to our rightful relationship with God as children of God. Amen!

BLACK & WHITE

Living life according to plan

E = Edify---Chapter 6

Therefore comfort each other and 'Edify' one another, just as you also are doing. 1 Thessalonians 5:11 (NKJV)

Let us always 'Edify' one another in the wisdom, knowledge and understanding of our Creator. (KS)

In John 14:6 Jesus says to us, "*I am the way, the truth, and the life. No one can come to the Father except through me.*" Yes, I often use this verse, but if we are to 'Edify' correctly that of moral and 'Biblical' knowledge, upholding the faith and holiness of the scriptures, then repetitiveness can only confirm certainty.

Jesus is saying to us in John 14:6; there is no other way to get back in sync with God, but through me…Adam was disobedient causing eternal separation…but I have been obedient and while you were yet sinners, I gave my life for you, making it possible for all to receive reconciliation with our Heavenly Father. *** In 1 Corinthians 15:22, Pauls says; (NIV) "For as in Adam all die, so in Christ all will be made alive."

What about edification of MORAL KNOWLEDGE?

Thinking of the word 'MORAL' I automatically reflect on where our laws came from…'Thou shall not murder' or 'Thou shall not steal'… or question our date calendar and the seven days a week. In six days, God created the heavens and the earth in their entire vast array, and on the seventh day He made it holy and rested…thus our seven days a week.
Perhaps we should allow God to direct our morals as well!

Yes, I'm one to keep it simple, as the essentials of God's word are simple.

BLACK & WHITE

Living life according to plan

E = Edify---Chapter 6

Therefore comfort each other and 'Edify' one another, just as you also are doing. 1 Thessalonians 5:11 (NKJV)

Let us always 'Edify' one another in the wisdom, knowledge and understanding of our Creator. (KS)

Webster's 1828 dictionary says that 'MORAL' is relating to the practice, manners or conduct of men as social beings in relation to each other, and with reference to right and wrong.

The word 'MORAL' is applicable to actions that are good or evil, virtuous or vicious, and has reference to the law of God as the standard by which their character is to be determined. The word however may be applied to actions, which affect only, or primarily and principally, a person's own happiness.

We might also think of moral character; moral views; moral knowledge; moral sentiments; moral maxims; moral approbation; moral doubts; moral justice; moral virtue; and/or moral obligations.

'MORAL' sense, an innate or natural sense of right and wrong; an instinctive perception of what is right or wrong in moral conduct, which approves some actions and disapproves others…

'MORAL' philosophy, the science of manners and duty; the science which treats of the nature and condition of man as a social being, of the duties which result from his social relations, and the reasons on which they are founded.

Should we be striving for 'MORAL' excellence, absolutely!

E = Edify---Chapter 6

Therefore comfort each other and 'Edify' one another, just as you also are doing. 1 Thessalonians 5:11 (NKJV)

Let us always 'Edify' one another in the wisdom, knowledge and understanding of our Creator. (KS)

In 2 Peter 1:5-8, Peter clearly enlightens us by saying that a life of 'MORAL' excellence leads to knowing God better. "5 So make every effort to apply the benefits of these promises to your life. Then your faith will produce a life of 'MORAL' excellence. A life of 'MORAL' excellence leads to knowing God better. 6 Knowing God leads to self-control. Self-control leads to patient endurance, and patient endurance leads to godliness. 7 Godliness leads to love for other Christians, and finally you will grow to have genuine love for everyone. 8 The more you grow like this; the more you will become productive and useful in your knowledge of our Lord Jesus Christ."

Do you suppose that as we learn to 'Edify' one another in the area of morals that a scriptural foundation is the best place to work from?

I believe the moral foundation of our world today came from the Holy Bible, the Judeo-Christian faith and not from anywhere or anything else. It is provable within reason, and we have just read from scripture what God teaches, and we know He grants us free will, to believe it or not. So individually, we are left with a choice to make; *Stand for the non-partisan morals of God that never change, and are fair for all…Or stand for the ever-changing biased morals of the world*!

E = Edify---Chapter 6

Therefore comfort each other and 'Edify' one another, just as you also are doing. 1 Thessalonians 5:11 (NKJV)

Let us always 'Edify' one another in the wisdom, knowledge and understanding of our Creator. (KS)

What about edification of RELIGIOUS KNOWLEDGE?

Having a 'Religion' is being 'Religious', with which I am not in favor of. To say I am 'Religious' could mean any number of things, including the incorporation of all religions and the gods and idolatry that go along with them. Let me explain!

Christianity is not a 'Religion' it's a 'RELATIONSHIP' with Christ.
When the word 'Religion' hits my ears I immediately think of, cults, many gods, something out there somewhere, Hollywood, extraterrestrial, Quija boards, re-incarnation, humming and/or emptying of our minds, dying and coming back as animals, statues and idols and countless other thoughts that an educated and civilized world should be smart enough to see as nothing more than fantasy, wild imaginations and humanistic effort at most for problem solving; not to mention, fear of God and truth.

How or why it is that truth and fact are shunned, while everything contrary is studied, worshiped and revered, boggles my mind. Apart from the absolute truth found in Christ, all that is seen as the big lie, appears as truth; satanic deception at work.

BLACK & WHITE

Living life according to plan

E = Edify---Chapter 6

Therefore comfort each other and 'Edify' one another, just as you also are doing. 1 Thessalonians 5:11 (NKJV)

Let us always 'Edify' one another in the wisdom, knowledge and understanding of our Creator. (KS)

I've said this before, that the Christian faith, a relationship with Jesus Christ is the only belief system that can support itself scientifically, geologically, historically, mathematically, archaeologically, including the area of cosmology. Nothing from the Holy Bible has ever been proven to be wrong; questioned and challenged yes, yet, something more significant is added daily to support its case -- www.creationmoments.com & www.answersingenesis.org, come to mind as two perfect examples to refute evolution hands down.

Man is one pathetic, proud, egotistical and immoral clown in desperate need of a 'Savior'... and yet, with all the technological power and information before him, he continues to run in the opposite direction of the very answer with the power to save him. How foolish we are!

Yours truly was once this pathetic, proud, egotistic and immoral clown, still a sinner, though saved by grace, who was constantly messing up his life and everyone else's around him for the first twenty-nine years.

No, I wasn't a murderer...an alcoholic...a drug addict...or a child molester...**I WAS FAR WORSE**! I am a three-time married man who was self-centered, full of pride, egotistical, unfaithful, inconsiderate, and full of nothing but worldly wisdom and self; 'Young and the useless' and the world to a tee!

BLACK & WHITE

Living life according to plan

E = Edify---Chapter 6

Therefore comfort each other and 'Edify' one another, just as you also are doing. 1 Thessalonians 5:11 (NKJV)

Let us always 'Edify' one another in the wisdom, knowledge and understanding of our Creator. (KS)

I was the kind of guy, through the example set that turns others into murderers, alcoholics and drug addicts, because of not being the husband, father, or leader that God called me and other men to be. I was doing more talking than listening, and literally, becoming all talk and no action, choosing the wisdom of the created over that of the Creator; wrong, very wrong (hindsight is twenty-twenty). 'Religion' cannot save us, but a relationship with Jesus Christ can.

Now you might be thinking: "but I'm a good man…I'm a good woman…good spouse, parent, friend, colleague, neighbor, and I have everything under control." But do you really?

Let me ask you…"what do you believe in?" You've heard me say before, when we stand for nothing we fall for anything…so "what is it you believe?"

We need a Savior, whether we want to admit it or not. We are not perfect, but if we do not know where we are going how can we get there?

If you say you are going to heaven and you have not accepted Jesus Christ as your personal Lord and Savior, then I hate to be the bearer of bad news, but you are not going to heaven without Christ in your heart! There is only one certain way to heaven known to man; (John 3:7/14:6).

E = Edify---Chapter 6

Therefore comfort each other and 'Edify' one another, just as you also are doing. 1 Thessalonians 5:11 (NKJV)

Let us always 'Edify' one another in the wisdom, knowledge and understanding of our Creator. (KS)

Probably two thirds or higher of the people in today's church congregations have heard about Jesus, but don't know him personally. Too many churches are into 'religion' and not Christ and Him crucified, and our need for an ongoing personal relationship with Him.

I could go on for hours and complicate things and confuse you into shutting down your brain, but please catch this; for you, or as you 'Edify' another, always keep your teaching simple and keep the following point a priority: 'Religion' cannot and will not save you---but a relationship with Jesus Christ can (See Romans 10:9)...that simple!

A brief definition of 'Religion' from Webster's 1828 dictionary reads: RELIGION - This word seems originally to have signified an oath or vow to the gods, or the obligation of such an oath or vow, which was held very sacred by the Romans.]

[**Personal perspective**]---"an oath or idol gods are not going to save us…and the Romans had hundreds of so called 'Religions'…as did Mohammed, founder of the Muslim faith, who pieced together the Quran from 360 different religions in his time, deciding on the 'moon god' of that day, 'Allah,' to be the god of 'his' Quran." (Human Accomplishment). Religion is complicated and being saved through Christ is easy...see again Romans 10:9 or John 3:16...simple, simple!

E = Edify---Chapter 6

Therefore comfort each other and 'Edify' one another, just as you also are doing. 1 Thessalonians 5:11 (NKJV)

Let us always 'Edify' one another in the wisdom, knowledge and understanding of our Creator. (KS)

'Religion', in its most comprehensive sense, includes a belief in the being and perfections of God, in the revelation of his will to man, in man's obligation to obey his commands, in a state of reward and punishment, and in man's accountableness to God; and also true godliness or piety of life, with the practice of all moral duties. It therefore comprehends theology, as a system of doctrines or principles, as well as practical piety; for the practice of moral duties... without a belief in a divine lawgiver, and without reference to his will or commands, is not religion.

[**Personal perspective**]---"sadly enough, the Being and perfections of God are now questioned, as perhaps being nothing more than myths, fables, and old wives tales... and 'Religion' today is without belief in a divine lawgiver, and without reference to His will."

As for faith and holiness of the Lord and His scriptures, it is essential as we 'Edify' others, that they understand it's ok to have questions about their belief. Having questions or at the least, believing in something is one thing--but being an atheist, believing in nothing, which is one's right to do so, is yet, unwise indeed. The fool says in his heart, "There is no God" (Psalm 14:1).

BLACK & WHITE

Living life according to plan

E = Edify---Chapter 6

Therefore comfort each other and 'Edify' one another, just as you also are doing. 1 Thessalonians 5:11 (NKJV)

Let us always 'Edify' one another in the wisdom, knowledge and understanding of our Creator. (KS)

Many believe in providence, the divine intervention of God that overcomes an individual when it's time for that person to step up to the plate, be noticed, and to make a difference.

In John 6:44 Jesus says: ... "For people can't come to me unless the Father who sent me draws them to me." Therefore, if you find yourself pondering spiritual thoughts, or feeling that something is missing in your life...or perhaps you're questioning the actual 'being' of God...or if someone has brought up their religion that you are wondering about, then perhaps this is what Jesus is talking about in John 6:44.

Perhaps 'God' is in action and His divine intervention has perked your curiosity enough to get you asking serious questions. He always has a reason for doing so.

There are literally hundreds of paths we can take to get our questions answered...but trust Him on this...not me or anyone or anything else; you are not reading this book by accident...are you?

To 'Edify' one in the 'Faith' of Christ, is to hear a blind person say, "I was blind, but now I see."

E = Edify---Chapter 6

Therefore comfort each other and 'Edify' one another, just as you also are doing. 1 Thessalonians 5:11 (NKJV)
Let us always 'Edify' one another in the wisdom, knowledge and understanding of our Creator. (KS)

Webster's 1828 dictionary says of 'Faith':

[FAITH is to persuade…to draw towards any 'thing'…to conciliate…to believe…to obey.

Evangelical, justifying, or saving faith, is the assent of the mind to the truth of divine revelation, on the authority of God's testimony, accompanied with a cordial assent of the will or approbation of the heart; an entire confidence or trust in God's character and declarations, and in the character and doctrines of Christ, with an unreserved surrender of the will to his guidance, and dependence on his merits for salvation. In other words, that firm belief of God's testimony, and of the truth of the gospel, which influences the will, and leads to an entire reliance on Christ for salvation.]

We have been justified by 'Faith'. Romans 5:1
Without 'Faith' it is impossible to please God. Hebrews 11:6
For we walk by 'Faith', and not by sight. 2 Corinthians 5:7

To 'Edify' one in the 'Holiness' of our Lord would be a lifetime asset for the recipient… a righteous gift to all who accept.

E = Edify---Chapter 6

Therefore comfort each other and 'Edify' one another, just as you also are doing. 1 Thessalonians 5:11 (NKJV)

Let us always 'Edify' one another in the wisdom, knowledge and understanding of our Creator. (KS)

Webster's 1828 dictionary says of 'Holiness':

[HO'LINESS (from holy) --- The state of being holy; freedom from sin; sanctity; Applied to the Supreme Being, holiness denotes perfect purity or integrity of moral character, one of His essential attributes.
Who is like thee, glorious in holiness? Exodus 15:11

Applied to human beings, 'Holiness' is purity of heart or dispositions; sanctified affections; piety; moral goodness, but not perfect…Piety in principle is a compound of veneration or reverence of the Supreme Being and love of His character, or veneration accompanied with love; and piety in practice, is the exercise of these affections in obedience to His will and devotion to His service. Piety is the only proper and adequate relief of decaying man.]

What better edification than to 'Edify' in the word of truth!

W = Work---Chapter 7

'Work' with enthusiasm, as though you were working for the Lord rather than for people. Ephesians 6:7 (NLT)

When we take Him to 'Work', 'Work' becomes fun. (KS)

I'm extremely excited about this chapter because God has provided me a whole new angle to 'Work' from…Get it! …Ok, so I'm a card at times, but I confess…it's all Him, 24/7*365.

Before jumping in as usual, I want you to know that I respect and admire you for seeking God's will, even if primarily curiosity at this particular point in time.

I may not know you personally, but I do in the Christian Spirit. Your heart is beating, and your blood is as red and flowing as distinctly as mine, as God leads us according to His specific calling for each of us.

I also want you to know how important of a step you have taken to follow the integrity of Jesus Christ. We can speak with anyone on the face of this planet, a government leader, the Queen of England, Donald Trump or a Bill Gates, but nothing from their lips can compare to chatting with the CEO of our universe, anytime, anywhere; we talk, He listens, and responds in His grace and mercy.

If you're not yet a Christian, I want to encourage you to keep reading and trusting in your heart. What you will begin to discover is that anyone who genuinely follows Christ, strives to live like Him …transparent, honest, and sincere, with love for everyone.

W = Work---Chapter 7

'Work' with enthusiasm, as though you were working for the Lord rather than for people. Ephesians 6:7 (NLT)

When we take Him to 'Work', 'Work' becomes fun. (KS)

And did I mention that in Him are hidden all the treasures of wisdom and knowledge? (Colossians 2:3)

Now together, let us experience 'Work' in a whole new light.

In retrospect, we've chosen thus far, to take up the 'Yoke' of God, to learn His ideals, who then continues to be our 'Overseer' we so desperately need, enabling us to live in 'Unity' with others, understanding the importance to 'Abstain' from all unrighteousness and our need to 'Repent' of our sins, as we grow to 'Edify' others, while continuing to appreciate and grow in absolute truth and fact.

We're now blessed with yet another benefit, a newly engineered passion for the 'Work' we do, which in turn, takes us on a much deeper and more rewarding journey, as we begin to gravitate to a much bigger 'Work' that lies within, as our ultimate purpose.

In other words, prior to this surprising change, when you may have found yourself complaining or not favoring your 'Work' place, you find your reactions completely the opposite, enjoying and being far more content and thorough in your 'Work' tasks and challenges, unlike before. Why?

For me, it was like night and day. One minute I was chasing a dream I always thought I wanted, and the next, couldn't care less.

BLACK & WHITE

Living life according to plan

W = Work---Chapter 7

'Work' with enthusiasm, as though you were working for the Lord rather than for people. Ephesians 6:7 (NLT)

When we take Him to 'Work', 'Work' becomes fun. (KS)

From TNN, to Health-Care, to being a Pastor, serious multiple Business failures, Author, and Speaker, has been an exciting and eye opening adventure to say the least.

One of Webster's 1828 dictionary definitions of 'Work', states…

--- [To labor is to be occupied in performing manual labor, whether severe or moderate. One man works better than another; one man works hard, another works lazily.]

The renowned department store tycoon, **J. C. Penney**, once quoted: "*Give me a stock clerk with a goal and I will give you a man who will make history…give me a man without a goal and I will give you a stock clerk.*"

There's a lot of truth in Mr. Penney's statement, and goals are important, and I believe in them. However I also believe in the majority of cases that many goals are written down before we talk them over with God. Therefore from the get-go we have the wrong motives, on the wrong path, with unmatched talents and gifts.

If you asked ten employees if they truly enjoyed their current line of work, you'd be pressed to find three to honestly say they do.

BLACK & WHITE

Living life according to plan

W = Work---Chapter 7

'Work' with enthusiasm, as though you were working for the Lord rather than for people. Ephesians 6:7 (NLT)

When we take Him to 'Work', 'Work' becomes fun. (KS)

Makes me think of James 4:2 & 3 ..."*the reason you don't have what you want is that you don't ask God for it. And even when you do ask, you don't get it because your whole motive is wrong*."

As an example, I spent twenty-three years chasing what I thought I always wanted in life, only to get there and be asking myself, what am I doing this for and for whom am I doing it?

I never once asked God what He wanted from me...probably and sadly enough because I never knew Him for the first twenty-nine years of my life. I'm not making excuses, just confessing a fact.

Now I know hindsight is 20/20, but honestly, I have pondered the thought, 'what if?' What if I had of known God sooner in my life and had asked Him what He had in mind for me? What changes or differences could I have made by this very day for my family, my community or myself? Of course, if the path were changed, so then would everything about me; would we really want to turn back time?

Insurmountable knowledge has come my way since the fall of 1987, as a born again Christian, appreciating that every step I've taken in life was all factored in as part of God's plan for me. And over the course of those years they have proven to be far superior in wisdom, knowledge and understanding than that of the first twenty-nine...but not without waves.

W = Work---Chapter 7

'Work' with enthusiasm, as though you were working for the Lord rather than for people. Ephesians 6:7 (NLT)

When we take Him to 'Work', 'Work' becomes fun. (KS)

What I'm getting at goes far beyond what we could possibly comprehend. When I mentioned above about the thought of knowing God sooner in my life, although all part of His ultimate plan, what I was referring to was our need as a global society to turn back to our Creator, and the younger and sooner the better.

So what does this have to do with the word 'Work?'... Everything!

God is the One who divinely designed us in our mother's womb, and He did so with a specific purpose in mind for each of us.

In Jeremiah 1:4-5 we read...4 "The Lord gave me a message. He said, 5 "I knew you before I formed you in your mother's womb. Before you were born I set you apart and appointed you as my spokesman to the world."And God says to Jeremiah in Jeremiah 29:11... "For I know the plans I have for you," says the Lord. "They are plans for good and not for disaster, to give you a future and a hope."

Thus, this has everything to do with 'Work', considering our desire is to get up in the morning and remain excited throughout the day before us.

When we humble ourselves before God and say to Him, "Lord, show me what it is you want me to do", the result is anything but disappointment.

BLACK & WHITE

Living life according to plan

W = Work---Chapter 7

'Work' with enthusiasm, as though you were working for the Lord rather than for people. Ephesians 6:7 (NLT)

When we take Him to 'Work', 'Work' becomes fun. (KS)

Our desire to do His 'Work' (our true purpose) is unquenchable.
Christ says to us in Matthew 7:7-8… 7 "Keep on asking, and you will be given what you ask for. 8 For everyone who asks, receives."

The PASSION of Christ is the passion we need to discover the real us.

Since He created us, does it not make perfect sense that He would know us best…our strengths and weaknesses considered?

We cannot help but wake up with passion, determination and focus, when His very lifeblood and dream that awaits within each of us is unleashed for His ultimate purpose and our well being.

AS AN EXAMPLE: Let's say you're now a plumber, but you're wired to be a carpenter. You're unable to get the full satisfaction of work because you're wired for driving nails, sawing boards and being engulfed in the aroma of cedar, pine or spruce…not repairing and/or installing water lines; plumbing's great, but not for you.

Or perhaps you're a Doctor, but God has you programmed for spiritual needs rather than health care needs. Again, chances of you experiencing peek, career exhilaration are slim to none, because you're programmed to go deeper emotionally and psychologically…you need much more.

W = Work---Chapter 7

'Work' with enthusiasm, as though you were working for the Lord rather than for people. Ephesians 6:7 (NLT)

When we take Him to 'Work', 'Work' becomes fun. (KS)

Do you see what I'm saying? God knows you and I better than anyone. He made us! He has us fine-tuned to His network and the signal will only come through at full capacity when we have the dial set to His channel.

ANOTHER EXAMPLE…if I'm singing country music, but God has me wired to sing Gospel, or other plans all together, my soul will remain restless until it finds its rest in His intended purpose for me…which was clearly not music; and I spent 23 years chasing it.

My friends, you and I are the cream-de-le-crème, wonderfully and masterfully made, wired into perfection and led to be humble. God, and God only, can know what is best for us. He knows what makes us tick; who knows the clock best...the retailer or its builder?

Choosing to take up the 'Yoke' of God is where the rubber meets the road and the excitement begins…where the adrenaline kicks in to overdrive, leaving us bright eyed, long into the wee hours of the night, or out of bed, dressed and pen in hand before the rooster crows.

A 'GODLY' man cannot be kept down. You're thinking, "But wait a minute, some of the biggest whiners, complainers and most unhappy people I know are Christians." Hey, I've been there, but only when I'm out of touch/fellowship, with the true King of Kings; ***if you're whining and complaining and/or unhappy, it's you/me, not God.***

BLACK & WHITE

Living life according to plan

W = Work---Chapter 7

'Work' with enthusiasm, as though you were working for the Lord rather than for people. Ephesians 6:7 (NLT)

When we take Him to 'Work', 'Work' becomes fun. (KS)

Once you sincerely invite Christ to lead your life the Potters wisdom, knowledge and understanding begins to envelope and molds us into shape. Over time, old thought patterns are replaced with new ones.

We can read in 2 Corinthians 5:17 where it says… "Therefore if anyone is in Christ, he is a new creation; the old has gone, the new has come."

WARNING! PLEASE DO NOT DO AS I DID. DON'T ASSUME YOU WON'T LIKE WHAT GOD WANTS FOR YOU. TRUST HIM!

The world is in the mess it is in for lack and use of Creator wisdom. "*It is impossible to rightly govern the world without God and the Holy Bible*," as quoted by George Washington.

The 'Cross and Him Crucified' is, always has been, and always will be, the essential ingredient needed for every man, woman and child, should they desire to secure their eternal salvation, by way of Christ, for which there is no other way. (John 14:6)

Apart from God, the world stands on its own wisdom, continuing to set priorities against God's ideals, while watching itself sink deeper and deeper into immorality...a million times over the sadness of Sodom and Gomorrah ever thought of being.

BLACK & WHITE

Living life according to plan

W = Work---Chapter 7

'Work' with enthusiasm, as though you were working for the Lord rather than for people. Ephesians 6:7 (NLT)

When we take Him to 'Work', 'Work' becomes fun. (KS)

God's priorities are as simple as one, two, three and four.

God needs to come first in life, so that we receive our guidance from the Creator and not the created; would you take your 'Ford' to the 'Pontiac' dealership for service, of course not!

The family slides in at third place, even before our 'Work/Career' which falls into the fourth position.

But there was no mention of number two! Oh yes, sliding into second place, cautiously and humbly, is '**self**'; if you don't like yourself, the person looking back at you in the mirror, then God is not first.

When we show obedience, putting Christ first, the self will mold into shape pretty quick, as will our family according to His plan. He then provides us our 'Work/Career' driven by passion, and not out of necessity, setting our hearts afire with a drive and determination, unique and specific to our own personal purpose and DNA makeup.

I remember while back in school and working part time at a gas bar, and in the midst of requiring a few references for a particular project, I provided the name of my part time employer, Mike, the owner. A few days later I was told my references were more than adequate but curiosity was raised about Mike's feedback.

BLACK & WHITE

Living life according to plan

W = Work---Chapter 7

'Work' with enthusiasm, as though you were working for the Lord rather than for people. Ephesians 6:7 (NLT)

When we take Him to 'Work', 'Work' becomes fun. (KS)

When asked what kind of person I was, Mike responded by saying, "*He's the only one I've ever known who whistles and sings in the rain while pumping gas.*"

It's not about me; it's about God! When He gets hold of us, life changes in more ways than we know. Fun replaces the pressures and the downsides of life. Although they still exist, they are miraculously removed from having any further control over us and taken care of in sufficient time.

Jesus says in Matthew 11:28: "Come to me, all of you who are weary and carry heavy burdens, and I will give you rest" … What can I say other than…He never fails to do what He promises to do...'IF'...we are willing to follow and trust in Him and not in ourselves; fair enough!

True enthusiasm and passion for our 'Work', is a gift from God. When we seek His will for our lives, putting Christ first, we are brought into harmony, in tune with Him, adding a whole new meaning to 'Work'.

God bless your journey!

Pssst…did I say thank you for being a 'Godly' influence?

O = Obey---Chapter 8

I've promised it once, and I'll promise it again: I will 'Obey' your righteous regulations. Psalm 119:106 (NLT)
Who better to 'Obey', than 'He' who created all (KS)

According to Webster's 1828 dictionary 'Obey' is…'To comply with the commands, orders or instructions of a superior…or with the requirements of law…moral, political or municipal; to do that which is commanded or required, or to forbear doing the prohibited.'

In Ephesians 6:1-3 we read…
1 Children, obey your parents because you belong to the Lord, for this is
the right thing to do. 2 Honor your father and mother." This is the first
commandment with a promise: 3 If you honor your father and mother,
"things will go well for you, and you will have a long life on the earth.

And in Colossians 3:22-23 we read, (Ad-libbing in brackets)…
22 You slaves (employees) must 'Obey' your earthly masters (bosses) in
everything you do. Try to please them all the time, not just when they are
watching you. 'Obey' them willingly because of your reverent fear
(worship) of the Lord. 23 Work hard and cheerfully at whatever you do,
as though you were working for the Lord rather than for people.

Paul tells us in Romans 6:17 (NIV), "But thanks be to God that, though you used to be slaves to sin, you have come to obey from your heart the pattern of teaching that has now claimed your allegiance."

Do we actually prefer death to life eternally?

BLACK & WHITE

Living life according to plan

O = Obey---Chapter 8

I've promised it once, and I'll promise it again: I will 'Obey' your righteous regulations. Psalm 119:106 (NLT)

Who better to 'Obey', than 'He' who created all (KS)

Rules and laws are like the Ten Commandments…they are not suggestions, but rather commandments, specific precepts for us to live by, established by God.

In Romans 6:16 it says, "Don't you realize that you become the slave of whatever you choose to obey? You can be a slave to sin, which leads to death, or you can choose to obey God, which leads to righteous living."

We are to raise our children up in the wisdom, knowledge and understanding of our Lord. **Just as the horse is needed to lead the cart, so it is that the Creator must lead the created**.

God gives us the choice to 'Obey', or not to 'Obey' (Deuteronomy 28)!

Deuteronomy 6:5-7 says: 5 Love the Lord your God with all your heart and with all your soul and with all your strength. 6 These commandments that I give you today are to be upon your hearts. 7 Impress them on your children. Talk about them when you sit at home and when you walk along the road, when you lie down and when you get up.

Also in Proverbs 22:6, (ESV) we read, "Train up a child in the way he should go; even when he is old he will not depart from it."

BLACK & WHITE

Living life according to plan

O = Obey---Chapter 8

I've promised it once, and I'll promise it again: I will 'Obey' your righteous regulations. Psalm 119:106 (NLT)

Who better to 'Obey', than 'He' who created all (KS)

As a young boy my dad would often caution me as for the need to 'Obey' all his rules; he was not a Christian man. As an illustration, I was told not to be poking a stick into the honeybee's nest found at the front of my Grandpa's garage (formerly a Holiness Church). Should I choose to disobey, I would suffer the consequences…in more ways than one.

About 1964, I learned the hard way that the best choice a child can make is to 'Obey'. First, in disobeying my dad, I found my *behind* suddenly warmer than usual. And second, the occupant honeybees decided this little two-legged nuisance was worth dying for; like Jesus dying for His children, they died for theirs...Ouch! (Honeybees sting once and die).

God questions Jerusalem about obeying Him in Isaiah 45: 9, 11, 12, 13:
9 "What sorrow awaits those who argue with their Creator. Does a clay pot argue with its maker? Does the clay dispute with the one who shapes it, saying, 'Stop, you're doing it wrong!' Does the pot exclaim, 'How clumsy can you be?' 11 This is what the LORD says— the Holy One of Israel and your Creator: "Do you question what I do for my children? Do you give me orders about the work of my hands? 12 I am the one who made the earth and created people to live on it. With my hands I stretched out the heavens. All the stars are at my command. 13 I will raise up Cyrus to fulfill my righteous purpose, and I will guide his actions. He will restore my city and free my captive people— without seeking a reward! I, the LORD of Heaven's Armies, have spoken!"

O = Obey---Chapter 8

I've promised it once, and I'll promise it again: I will 'Obey' your righteous regulations. Psalm 119:106 (NLT)

Who better to 'Obey', than 'He' who created all (KS)

I guess if I'm for Him, then I too must be bold where boldness is needed.

To 'Obey' is wise. To disobey is unwise…not rocket science!
Proverbs 12:15 says, "Fools think their own way is right, but the wise listen to others."

Paul teaches us in Galatians 6:7 that we reap what we sow; if we sow the seeds of servant-hood, humbleness, kindness, gentleness and the likes, while choosing to seek God's wisdom, knowledge and understanding, it's fair to say we can expect to reap the rewards for being obedient.
David says in Psalm 37:4, "Take delight in the Lord, and he will give you the desires of your heart."

On the contrary, if we sow selfishness, obscenities, pride, arrogance and the likes, while choosing to hang with fools, accepting their wisdom, over that of the Creator, then it's also fair to say we can expect to reap the rewards of being disobedient, with exceptions, but most definitely not without consequences.

James says in James 1:22, (NIV) "Do not merely listen to the word, and so deceive yourselves; Do what it says." ... On another note, Proverbs 13:20 tells us, "Walk with the wise and become wise, for a companion of fools suffers harm."

BLACK & WHITE

Living life according to plan

O = Obey---Chapter 8

I've promised it once, and I'll promise it again: I will 'Obey' your righteous regulations. Psalm 119:106 (NLT)

Who better to 'Obey', than 'He' who created all (KS)

Let me ask you…if we play with fire is there a slight possibility that we will get burned? I'm being somewhat facetious, I know!

If we read in the book of Genesis 19:1-26, we not only find the reason for the destruction of Sodom and Gomorrah, the very act of Sodomy, deliberate disobedience to the Laws of God, we also see Lot's wife, exercising her personal desires and refusing to 'Obey' her husband and more importantly, the lordship of Yahweh. She was more interested in material possessions than in spiritual truths and as a result of ignoring to 'Obey' a direct order, and while knowing some form of punishment would follow for looking back, she chose to do so anyway and was immediately turned into a pillar of salt. (V-26)

We can look to Shadrach, Meshach and Abednego in Daniel 3:19-30, where by the grace of God, through their obedience to 'Obey' and hold fast to their faith in the living God, they walked out from the flames of an excruciating fire without a mark or sweat bead on them, in witness to the formerly hostile King Nebuchadnezzar, who suddenly had a change of heart after what he saw and became tame, forgiving and supportive of their faith and in their living God.

Or how about Daniel, being thrown into the lion's den under wrongful and envious accusations, (Daniel 6) because he chose to stand firm and 'Obey' his God.

BLACK & WHITE

Living life according to plan

O = Obey---Chapter 8

I've promised it once, and I'll promise it again: I will 'Obey' your righteous regulations. Psalm 119:106 (NLT)

Who better to 'Obey', than 'He' who created all (KS)

Daniel walked out of the den without a scratch or wound, (V-23) and witnessed King Darius saying to his people, 'in every part of my Kingdom, people must fear and reverence the God of Daniel (V-26) … He has rescued Daniel from the power of the lions.' (V-27)

Or how about when Jesus is describing the difference between a truly sold out disciple and one that is make believe? He states in Matthew 7:21, "Not everyone who says to me, 'Lord, Lord,' will enter the kingdom of heaven, but only the one who does the will of my Father who is in heaven."

Jesus goes on to say that many will believe until the last minute they have hit the homerun to win them a seat in eternity, but on judgment day He will be saying to them, "I never knew you, go away!" (V-23)

Obedience is everything we need…and it's found in God and the Holy Bible. John 1:1-5 says it best. **1** In the beginning was the Word, and the Word was with God, and the Word was God. **2** He was with God in the beginning. **3** Through him all things were made; without him nothing was made that has been made. **4** In him was life, and that life was the light of all mankind. **5** The light shines in the darkness, and the darkness has not overcome it.

BLACK & WHITE

Living life according to plan

O = Obey---Chapter 8

I've promised it once, and I'll promise it again: I will 'Obey' your righteous regulations. Psalm 119:106 (NLT)

Who better to 'Obey', than 'He' who created all (KS)

The wisest and wealthiest to ever live concludes his book of Ecclesiastes 12:13-14 with the following:13 "*Fear God and obey his commands, for this is the duty of every person.* 14 *God will judge us for everything we do, including every secret thing, whether good or bad*."

When Jesus is asked, in Mark 12:28, "Of all the commandments, which is the most important?"… He responds in verses 29-31 by saying:
29 "The most important commandment is this: 'Hear, O Israel! The Lord our God is the one and only Lord. 30 And you must love the Lord your God with all your heart, all your soul, all your mind, and all your strength. 31 The second is equally important: 'Love your neighbor as yourself.' No other commandment is greater than these."

Paul, in the book of Romans 13:8-10, is led of the Holy Spirit to expand our understanding of just how important 'love' is and addresses it by saying:8 Pay all your debts, except the debt of love for others. You can never finish paying that! If you love your neighbor, you will fulfill all the requirements of God's law. 9 For the commandments against adultery and murder and stealing and coveting—and any other commandment—are all summed up in this one commandment: "Love your neighbor as yourself. 10 Love does no wrong to anyone, so love satisfies all of God's requirements.

Obedience to God's priorities must capture our full time attention.

R = Rejoice---Chapter 9

Therefore I 'Rejoice' that I have confidence in you in everything.
2 Corinthians 7:16 (NKJV)
I 'Rejoice' in God's grace, that I judge no one. (KS)

According to Noah Webster, 'Rejoice' is...
...To experience joy and gladness in a high degree: To be exhilarated with lively and pleasurable sensations: To exalt!

I'm going to be bold and jump right in to say that one of my favorite bible verses is...Psalm 9:14 (KJV) where it says, "I will 'Rejoice' in thy salvation". Wow, I'm living forever! Yes!

This simple act of faith, of being born again, to receive eternal salvation, saves and changes lives because God is real, God is love, and God is unconditionally forgiving to a sincere and repentant heart. Man can only be real, full of love and unconditionally forgiving of all who sin against him when God is in the picture...so 'Rejoice'!

In Luke 10:17 & 20 we read; 17 When the seventy-two disciples returned, they joyfully reported to him, (Jesus) "Lord, even the demons obey us when we use your name!" And Jesus replied, 20 But don't rejoice because evil spirits obey you; rejoice because your names are registered in heaven."

My friends, this is what David is boasting about in Psalm 118:24; "This is the day the LORD has made. We will rejoice and be glad in it."

BLACK & WHITE

Living life according to plan

R = Rejoice---Chapter 9

Therefore I 'Rejoice' that I have confidence in you in everything.
2 Corinthians 7:16 (NKJV)

I 'Rejoice' in God's grace, that I judge no one. (KS)

If I remember correctly, I saw Dr. Norman Vincent Peale when he was ninety-two, speaking in Laval, Quebec Canada in 1992. With energy to boot, matching that, if not more than the younger line up of speakers, he humbly overwhelmed his audience by way of his renowned simple and straightforward approach to the gospel and opened with, Psalm 118:24 as noted above. God rest his soul! What better man for God to have used to author 'The Power of Positive Thinking,' the very book that allowed me and millions of others to see Jesus Christ, the King of Kings in a completely different light; anything and everything but hell and damnation.

Dr. Peale then went on to share how his grandfather had said to him, "Norman, you have a choice in life to be happy or sad". "Which one do you suppose I chose?" he said to his audience. Of course the place filled with laughter. Dr. Peale was unquestionably a distinguished and personally handpicked leader for God indeed.

I bring Dr Peale's name to the table because I've heard the perfect Christian often condemn him for his 'positive thinking only' message. He was too this, or too that, and always missing the point apparently!

If anything, I believe Dr. Norman Vincent Peale is one of many who never, ever, missed the point and God used him to lead millions into the Kingdom, by way of his own personal DNA-Distinguished-Style.

R = Rejoice---Chapter 9

Therefore I 'Rejoice' that I have confidence in you in everything.
2 Corinthians 7:16 (NKJV)

I 'Rejoice' in God's grace, that I judge no one. (KS)

Dr. Peale, certainly walked the talk fulfilling the great commission found in Matthew 28, and praise God that he left no scandals behind to darken the Christian faith any more than it already was… and is today.

We have far more reason to 'Rejoice' than to complain or worry.

Take Psalm 23 for example:
1 The Lord is my shepherd; I have everything I need. 2 He lets me rest in
green meadows; he leads me beside peaceful streams. 3 He renews my
strength. He guides me along right paths, bringing honor to his name. 4
Even when I walk through the dark valley of death, I will not be afraid,
for you are close beside me. Your rod and your staff protect and comfort
me. 5 You prepare a feast for me in the presence of my enemies. You
welcome me as a guest, anointing my head with oil. My cup overflows
with blessings. 6 Surely your goodness and unfailing love will pursue me
all the days of my life, and I will live in the house of the Lord forever.

For me, it was surely comforting and worth 'Rejoicing' to know that with my one simple act of faith, to invite Jesus Christ into my life, to repent, in my case, twenty-nine years of sin off my shoulders and into His lap and to also receive 24/7 access to the CEO of our Universe.

His eternal gift in return is that He will remain my shepherd/overseer, providing me everything from rest, strength, guidance, protection, food and water and fill all my needs with endless blessings forever and ever.

R = Rejoice---Chapter 9

Therefore I 'Rejoice' that I have confidence in you in everything.
2 Corinthians 7:16 (NKJV)
I 'Rejoice' in God's grace, that I judge no one. (KS)

We need nothing more when Jesus Christ is leading our life!

The thought, that there is absolutely nothing He can't or won't do for us if we remain faithful to Him is beyond human understanding; not to mention the fact that He gave the word 'servant' a whole new meaning.

May I be so bold as to say that even when we backslide, He stands firm, unchanging, always loving us, and awaiting our desire to repent and restore our fellowship with Him.

But let us not puff up with pride and miss the warning Jesus provides us as He speaks of 'the Rich Man and Lazarus' in Luke 16:19-31. For illustrational purposes, let's look at verses, 20; 23; 31, of Luke 16, (NIV) which read as follows:

16:20 At his gate (the rich man's) was laid a beggar named Lazarus, covered with sores.

16:23 In hell, (Hades) where he (the rich man) was in torment, he looked up and saw Abraham far away, with Lazarus by his side.

16:31 And he (Abraham) said to him, "If they (the rich man's five brothers) do not listen to Moses and the Prophets, they will not be convinced even if someone rises from the dead.

R = Rejoice---Chapter 9

Therefore I 'Rejoice' that I have confidence in you in everything.
2 Corinthians 7:16 (NKJV)

I 'Rejoice' in God's grace, that I judge no one. (KS)

A couple of keen interest points here, is that because Jesus never used personal names in His parables, which He does here, (Lazarus) many commentators and scholars alike believe this story relates to actual events that take place (Luke 16:20).

Four factors involved with these three verses above are worthy of taking notice, because they provide believers and potential believers in Christ, the opportunity to appreciate the need for having our name in the Lamb's Book of Life…and all the more reason to 'Rejoice'.

Revelation 21:27 says; "Nothing evil will be allowed to enter (Heaven) —only those whose names are written in the Lamb's Book of Life."

So let us take a brief look at these four factors from Luke 16.

"**Begging**" (16:20) … The New Testament mentions several people who are forced by illness or disability to beg for survival (Luke 16:20, John 9:8, Acts 3:2-11). In the 1st Century and in rabbinical Judaism, giving to the destitute was considered a great deed, meritorious in God's eyes (Matthew 6:1-4)

"**In Hell**" (16:23) … The Greek word 'Hades' is a general term for the place inhabited by the eternal dead. This rich man didn't take the Gospel seriously and was evidently not in the Lamb's Book of Life.

R = Rejoice---Chapter 9

Therefore I 'Rejoice' that I have confidence in you in everything.
2 Corinthians 7:16 (NKJV)

I 'Rejoice' in God's grace, that I judge no one. (KS)

"Life after death" (16:23) … Not life - but alive! The now dead, rich man, is pictured as self-conscious, aware, and able to see, feel and remember.

There is no biblical basis for the notion that death is an unconscious state. The human personality is fully conscious and aware and does outlast physical death, according to Christ's illustration.

So who is suddenly rejoicing at the thought of being on Lazarus's side of the fence/chasm? … **Do I hear an Amen**?

Our last factor surrounding the Luke 16 example is heeding us to listen to God 'NOW.'

"Listen to God's word 'NOW." (16:31) … Jesus' sad observation that the rich man's brothers would not listen (i.e., respond, act on what they heard) even if one rose from the dead, was quickly proven true. Jesus was raised from the dead. But His enemies, determined not to believe, continued to reject Him.

All Christians should be 'Rejoicing?' Why? Jesus said to us in Luke 10:20; … "Rejoice because your names are registered as citizens of heaven."

BLACK & WHITE

Living life according to plan

R = Rejoice---Chapter 9

Therefore I 'Rejoice' that I have confidence in you in everything.
2 Corinthians 7:16 (NKJV)

I 'Rejoice' in God's grace, that I judge no one. (KS)

Jesus, is sharing with all people, every tribe and nation, to come to Him, to never want or thirst again, and to 'Rejoice' with Him that our names are written in the Lamb's Book of Life.

Yes, Kevin, but still, what's the big deal?

The big deal for 'Rejoicing' is that you will be joining Lazarus in heaven and not the rich man in hell for ignoring the truth. You will never see death! Bodily death yes...Spiritual death, no.

Jesus died on the cross, was buried and raised from the dead by His/our Heavenly Father, on the third day, thus defeating death. Therefore, when we confess that Jesus Christ is Lord, and believe that God raised Him from the dead, we also defeat death through Him.

The fact that we can kill the body, but cannot kill the soul is exciting for me and should also be for you.

The fact that a simple act of faith can take anyone, from death to life eternal is the kind of phenomenon that truly makes a difference.

The fact that God spoke the world into being, starting from a formless, empty and dark existence, with His Spirit hovering over nothing but water, in which He set the land upon that we walk today, is astounding beyond understanding.

R = Rejoice---Chapter 9

Therefore I 'Rejoice' that I have confidence in you in everything.
2 Corinthians 7:16 (NKJV)

I 'Rejoice' in God's grace, that I judge no one. (KS)

The fact that God created perfection, only to have to flush, destroy it, and start over, and then watch, as history repeated itself into further infectious degradation, holding fast to His covenant to never destroy by water again, while being too righteous and holy to lie or deceive, and remaining unconditionally forgiving throughout it all, is pretty good evidence that He is nothing short of being Omniscient, Omnipresent and Omnipotent, just as scripture proclaims.

My friends what possible reason is there for Christians not to 'Rejoice?' If our only evidence was Psalm 23, it is sufficient in pertinent information alone to place our trust and faith in Him and His Son Jesus Christ. God provides us the freedom to choose life or death. I find solid ground to personally 'Rejoice' in a living God who gives me the will to choose, and then accepts my fate with either rejoicing or with tears.

'Rejoicing' in the Lord is Paul's theme in the book of Philippians. The word 'Rejoice' occurs in the King James Bible (KJV) one hundred and ninety-two times, eleven of which we find in …Philippians 1:18, 2:16, 17, 18, & 28, 3:1 &3, and 4:4.

All of this 'Rejoicing' comes as a result of and through Christ. Paul says as he closes in on the end of Philippians 4:19 (NLT) … "And this same God who takes care of me will supply all your needs from his glorious riches, which have been given to us in Christ Jesus."

BLACK & WHITE

Living life according to plan

R = Rejoice---Chapter 9

Therefore I 'Rejoice' that I have confidence in you in everything.
2 Corinthians 7:16 (NKJV)

I 'Rejoice' in God's grace, that I judge no one. (KS)

Because of Christ and what He did for us, while we were yet sinners, we can and should 'Rejoice'.

No other gift on planet earth can suffice the gift of eternal life. We will literally close our eyes here and open them up there!

From a Pastoral perspective, we 'Rejoice' with John, in 2 John 1:4, and 3 John 1:3-4, (KJV) because he 'Rejoices' in the salvation of others…
2 John 1:4 "I rejoiced greatly that I found of thy children walking in truth, as we have received a commandment from the Father."
3 John 1:3-4 says: "For I rejoiced greatly, when the brethren came and testified of the truth that is in thee, even as thou walkest in the truth. I have no greater joy than to hear that my children walk in truth."

In the Book of Zephaniah, in spite of its underlying theme of judgment and punishment, the book ends with a glorious promise for the future.
As directed by God, Zephaniah 3:17 (NKJ) says… "The Lord your God in your midst, The Mighty One, will save; He will 'Rejoice' over you with gladness, He will quiet you with His love, He will 'Rejoice' over you with singing."

As the message of God remains unchanged and as we learn to make Him our first priority, only then do great things begin to happen for personal, family and business life.

R = Rejoice---Chapter 9

Therefore I 'Rejoice' that I have confidence in you in everything.
2 Corinthians 7:16 (NKJV)
I 'Rejoice' in God's grace, that I judge no one. (KS)

James 4:2 says, "You want what you don't have, so you scheme and kill to get it. You are jealous for what others have, and you can't possess it, so you fight and quarrel to take it away from them. And yet the reason you don't have what you want is that you don't ask God for it."

How many times have you or someone you know complained about what we don't have, forgetting the importance of what we do have? Greek philosopher Epicurus (341 BC - 270 BC)…said it this way…"He is a wise man who does not grieve for the things which he has not, but 'Rejoices' for those which he has."

Check this one out!

In 2 Corinthians 12:9, 10 (KJV) Paul says: …9-And he said unto me," My grace is sufficient for thee: for my strength is made perfect in weakness." Most gladly therefore will I rather glory in my infirmities, that the power of Christ may rest upon me. 10 Therefore I take pleasure in infirmities, in reproaches, in necessities, in persecutions, in distresses for Christ's sake: for when I am weak, then am I strong."

Certainly this is further proof and support for what Paul says earlier in 2 Corinthians 7:16 (NKJ) as noted at the top of this page.

BLACK & WHITE

Living life according to plan

R = Rejoice---Chapter 9

Therefore I 'Rejoice' that I have confidence in you in everything.
2 Corinthians 7:16 (NKJV)

I 'Rejoice' in God's grace, that I judge no one. (KS)

Paul learned to 'Rejoice' under all circumstances without complaint.

Author has learned to 'Rejoice' in His wisdom provided, as well as His discipline dished out (*80% of the time...I'm human*), thanks to Paul, for being faithful and loyal, documenting according to the leading of the Holy Spirit.

The armor of God is the word of God. Whether adventuring or defending, He is there to guide our steps when we seek His will.

When times are tough, we will marvel at how His grace is sufficient for us. When we are strong, He is there to make us stronger still. When we are weak, He lifts us up in the midst of it all.

Is it always a breeze because I can give it all to Him?

No! But I 'Rejoice' in knowing that I can lean on Him, 24/7, 365 days a year, resting assured that He will never leave me nor forsake me, because that is just one of His many promises to me, you, and all who trust in Him...the living God...King of Kings and Lord of Lords.

T = Tithe---Chapter 10

Jesus says, "You should tithe, yes, but do not neglect the more important things; justice, mercy, and faith." Matthew 23:23c (NLT)
To 'Tithe' is to love God more than money. (KS)

It is the most peculiar thing, when we take what we would normally claim to be our own, our paycheck, 'Tithe' one tenth of it to match hundreds or even thousands of other givers alike, in helping spread the greatest message ever to mankind, assuming we would then live with less ourselves, only to receive far more in return, often in our own time of need, all because we first gave to others.

God shares the Law of tithing in Deuteronomy 14:22 (NLT): "You must set aside a tithe of your crops—one-tenth of all the crops you harvest each year."

And the purpose of our tithing is shared in Deuteronomy 14:23 that reads, "The purpose of tithing is to teach you always to fear (worship) the Lord your God."

Here we have the President and CEO of our universe saying to us; "I have provided and will continue providing everything you need to earn a living, to put food on your table, clothe & provide shelter, and all I ask in return is ten cents from every dollar you generate."

We all must decide in our heart how much to give. And don't give reluctantly or in response to pressure. "For God loves a person who gives cheerfully." (2 Corinthians 9:7 - NLT).

BLACK & WHITE

Living life according to plan

T = Tithe---Chapter 10

Jesus says, "You should tithe, yes, but do not neglect the more important things; justice, mercy, and faith." Matthew 23:23c (NLT)

To 'Tithe' is to love God more than money. (KS)

Because tithing plays such an important role in our Christian stewardship, let us once again recap and see what you and I actually have at our fingertips as we put our trust in God's hands.

By the grace of the One who created us all and through the power of The Holy Spirit, you and I have taken up the 'Yoke' of God seriously, and chosen to learn from the true source of wisdom.

Immediately because of our actions, God takes us under His wing as our 24/7, 365 day-a-year 'Overseer', finding ourselves genuinely eager to live in 'Unity' with others out of appreciation for our distinctions and the exclusivity that God himself would ordain us all. What a humbling feeling to live sincerely outside of envy or jealousy or the likes of that which thrives in many minds and hearts of a hurting and truth seeking society.

By example, God makes it clear to us the need to live in 'Unity' with others, and to do so, we must have His understanding and need to 'Abstain' from all unrighteousness and to 'Repent' of all our sins, so that we may then 'Edify' others out of and in total righteousness, by example.

We must keep in mind that those who teach best are those who practice what they preach…which can be good or evil, agreed!

T = Tithe---Chapter 10

Jesus says, "You should tithe, yes, but do not neglect the more important things; justice, mercy, and faith." Matthew 23:23c (NLT)
To 'Tithe' is to love God more than money. (KS)

When God brings us to the point of edifying others, our lives must show evidence of serious change, such as being more focused and in tune with His purpose for us. Life becomes easier with Him in control, being void of worry and fear that weighs heavy on the shoulders of the unsaved soul. When God leads, problems disappear.

An example might be:

1/ knowing we have a bank loan on Monday, our pay on Friday is delayed, but we know God will meet our need …= God is in control … OR …
2/ …Same scenario but panic takes over, expecting loan to end in default …= God is not in control.

Continuing with God leading, our 'Work' has now miraculously lost its worldly mindset and taken on more of a servant-hood attitude. We find ourselves asking not what my work can do for me, but rather, what I can do for my work; owners, co-workers, those I support, etc.

As we have grown to walk in the Spirit of God we understand perfectly, whom to 'Obey' and whom not to 'Obey'. A true servant of God is humbled when rebuked and judged in truth, as they appreciate the fact that it can only add to their inspired knowledge of God.

T = Tithe---Chapter 10

Jesus says, "You should tithe, yes, but do not neglect the more important things; justice, mercy, and faith." Matthew 23:23c (NLT)
To 'Tithe' is to love God more than money. (KS)

Augustine, referring to those still living in the flesh quoted, "We like the truth when it informs us…we hate truth when it judges us."

When our eyes are opened and we experience this whole new way of thinking, acting, and being responsive and accountable to a higher power, we have clearly discovered good reason to 'Rejoice'.

God is with us***He oversees us***we have a peace of mind to live a life void of worldly ignorance of right from wrong***the desire to abstain from unrighteousness without the feeling of loss or judgment of others***the humbleness to repent of our wrongs and change for the good of all including ourselves***to be zealous in edifying others in discovering the same***determination to be a servant***and the wisdom and self-confidence to obey those who correct and direct according to God's ideals, and for that we do rejoice and are grateful.

And here in chapter ten (10), we have one of the most fundamental yet powerful concepts before us called *tithing* that needs to remain one of the central focuses of the church, as tithing plays an intricate and essential role in maintaining the spread of the Gospel worldwide; obviously, accountability plays a major role here as well.

At the top of this chapter you find a personal quote that reads, "To 'Tithe' is to love God more than money."

BLACK & WHITE

Living life according to plan

T = Tithe---Chapter 10

Jesus says, "You should tithe, yes, but do not neglect the more important things; justice, mercy, and faith." Matthew 23:23c (NLT)

To 'Tithe' is to love God more than money. (KS)

Too many Christian leaders are adopting a misleading doctrine; "Give and you will receive!" Too many of the wrong pockets are being filled; their calling it God's work, but only thievery is being accomplished.

I heard it said best while in Lynchburg, Virginia for their annual 'Super Conference' at Liberty University, when one of the many speakers, Ed Young Jr., Senior Pastor of Fellowship Church in the heart of the Dallas/Fort Worth area said, "*We don't give to receive, we receive to give.*"

The idea here that we actually receive from God, to give, could not have been addressed more appropriately or scripturally. There is nothing wrong with expecting fringe benefits in return for our tithes and offerings however, to teach the mindset that, 'If I give today, I can expect something perhaps today or tomorrow,' is misleading to any giver.

It's important we remember that all promises of God are fulfilled on His terms…not of man's. If God is willing, He will bless us.

All our giving and deeds are to be done in secret, with a cheerful heart and not grudgingly. God sees what is done in secret…and rewards us on His terms and in His timing.

BLACK & WHITE

Living life according to plan

T = Tithe---Chapter 10

Jesus says, "You should tithe, yes, but do not neglect the more important things; justice, mercy, and faith." Matthew 23:23c (NLT)

To 'Tithe' is to love God more than money. (KS)

Paul tells us in 2 Corinthians 9:7, (NKJ)... "So let each one give as he purposes in his heart, not grudgingly or of necessity; for God loves a cheerful giver."

Spiritual blessings don't flow to a bitter heart, or to fulfill selfish greed. Blessings flow rather, to those who genuinely love and desire to be good and faithful stewards in fulfilling God's word...all of it, to the best of our abilities; not pretending as though not knowing His true word.

Jesus tells us in Matthew 6:1-4 (NLT). 1 "Take heed that you do not do your charitable deeds before men, to be seen by them. Otherwise you have no reward from your Father in heaven. 2 Therefore, when you do a charitable deed, do not sound a trumpet before you as the hypocrites do in the synagogues and in the streets, that they may have glory from men. Assuredly, I say to you, they have their reward. 3 But when you do a charitable deed, do not let your left hand know what your right hand is doing, 4 that your charitable deed may be in secret; and your Father who sees in secret will Himself reward you openly."

The full revelation of God in the New Testament reveals that we are to practice one hundred percent stewardship (2Corinthians Chapter's 8 & 9).

T = Tithe---Chapter 10

Jesus says, "You should tithe, yes, but do not neglect the more important things; justice, mercy, and faith." Matthew 23:23c (NLT)
To 'Tithe' is to love God more than money. (KS)

In Matthew 23:23, Jesus boldly proclaims; "How terrible it will be for you teachers of religious law and you Pharisees. Hypocrites! For you are careful to 'Tithe' even the tiniest part of your income, but you ignore the important things of the law—justice, mercy, and faith. You should tithe, yes, but you should not leave undone the more important things."

Jesus makes it clear that stewardship must be 100%...not 50%, 80% or 99.9%...Above tithing, things like justice, mercy and faith need also apply in fulfilling honorable stewardship.

The exciting news is, when we 'Tithe' our 10% from everything we earn and give it to God, His church, and purposes, it makes available the finances necessary to spread the good news to every quarter of the earth via snail-mail and E-mail, radio, television, Holy Bible distribution, and hands-on missionaries.

By tithing, we are helping to fulfill 'The Great Commission' in Matthew 28:19, 20,"Therefore, go and make disciples of all the nations, baptizing them in the name of the Father and the Son and the Holy Spirit. Teach these new disciples to obey all the commands I have given you."

It costs money to spread the 'Good News,' as well as compensate our Pastors, who spend a minimum of 65 hours a week in visitation, counseling, and/or service preparation.

T = Tithe---Chapter 10

Jesus says, "You should tithe, yes, but do not neglect the more important things; justice, mercy, and faith." Matthew 23:23c (NLT)
To 'Tithe' is to love God more than money. (KS)

Our faithfulness also helps compensate the church secretary, fund mission trips, send children to Christian camps and events, pay for office and worship supplies, equipment and local outreach programs, not to mention electric bills, rent, hydro, etcetera, for accommodation upkeep.

Like anything else, it's endless to the expenses involved in getting and keeping all things running, especially, the good news circulating and making a difference.

God is worth it right! What better news to spread than the 'Good News' that is found in the greatest and most successful bestselling book ever; The Holy Bible?

Do you see what is happening here?

Because of our full obedience to God's word, the good news, the Gospel of Jesus Christ, is able to remain in the spotlight, making the world a better place, even for unbelievers…as intended. If we don't help fund the exploitation of good news, then bad news will simply take its place; *tell me, what do you see and hear about most...good or bad news*?

I thank God for your giving, and ask that He bless you abundantly according to His will and perfect timing.

T = Tithe---Chapter 10

Jesus says, "You should tithe, yes, but do not neglect the more important things; justice, mercy, and faith." Matthew 23:23c (NLT)
To 'Tithe' is to love God more than money. (KS)

As I bring this chapter to a close, let me leave you with a few thought provoking quotes.

Albert Einstein said; "The world is a dangerous place to live; not because of the people who are evil, but because of the people who do nothing about it."

Mathew D. Staver (Founder & President of Liberty Counsel) said; "Without morality, the foundations of our liberty will crumble because there will be no moral compass differentiating between right and wrong."

Kevin Simpson said; "Chasing money is the curse...having money is the freedom...knowing what to do with it is the blessing."

Your 'Tithe' plays a significant role as to who rules: God or satan.

H = Humble---Chapter 11

"'Humble' yourselves therefore under the mighty hand of God, that He may exalt you in due time." 1 Peter 5:6 (KJV)
To be 'Humble' is to invite exaltation. (KS)

After the purchase of his 1828 Dictionary on CD-Rom, curiosity left me intrigued to know more about the author. I soon discovered a distinguished and 'Humble' man by the name of Noah Webster, born October 16, 1758. He claimed to have coined only one word---'demoralize,' defined: "To corrupt or undermine the morals of; to destroy or lessen the effect of moral principles on; to render corrupt in morals."

Noah was the author of the first American dictionary, published in 1806 under the title of 'A Compendious Dictionary of the English Language.' He immediately went to work on his magnum opus, 'An American Dictionary of the English Language,' for which he learned twenty-six (26) languages, including Anglo-Saxon and Sanskrit, in order to research the origins of his own country's tongue…Thus…the birth of 'Webster's 1828 Dictionary' with an incredible 70,000 entries.

The G. & C. Merriam Co. of 1831, renamed Merriam-Webster Inc. in 1982, inherited the Webster legacy when the Merriam brothers, George and Charles, bought the unsold copies of the 1841 edition of 'An American Dictionary of the English Language, Corrected and Enlarged' from Webster's heirs after the death of Noah Webster in 1843.

With secured rights to create revised editions, Noah's work, renowned for its distinguished and Godly heritage appeal, was soon forgotten, resulting in today's watered-down and extremely vague versions.

H = Humble---Chapter 11

"'Humble' yourselves therefore under the mighty hand of God, that He may exalt you in due time." 1 Peter 5:6 (KJV)

To be 'Humble' is to invite exaltation. (KS)

Speaking of being 'Humble', Noah Webster in his renowned, 1828 Dictionary says this:

'Humble': [L. humilis.]

Lowly; modest; meek; submissive; opposed to proud, haughty, arrogant or assuming.
Thy 'Humble' nest built on the ground.
Low; opposed to lofty or great; mean; not magnificent; as a 'Humble' cottage.
A 'Humble' roof, and an obscure retreat.

In an evangelical sense, having a low opinion of one's self, and a deep sense of unworthiness in the sight of God.
God resisteth the proud, but giveth grace to the 'Humble'. James 4:6
Without a 'Humble' imitation of the divine author of our blessed religion, we can never hope to be a happy nation.

'Humble': to abase; to reduce to a low state. This victory humbled the pride of Rome. The power of Rome was humbled, but not subdued.
To crush; to break; to subdue. The battle of Waterloo [June 18, 1815] humbled the power of Bonaparte…as in, (Napoleon Bonaparte, born on August 15, 1769 in Ajaccio on the Mediterranean island of Corsica)

H = Humble---Chapter 11

"'Humble' yourselves therefore under the mighty hand of God, that He may exalt you in due time." 1 Peter 5:6 (KJV)

To be 'Humble' is to invite exaltation. (KS)

To make 'Humble' or lowly in mind; to abase the pride of; to reduce arrogance and self-dependence; to give a low opinion of one's moral worth; to make meek and submissive to the divine will; the evangelical sense.

'Humble' yourselves under the mighty hand of God, that he may exalt you. 1 Peter 5:6

Hezekiah humbled himself for the pride of his heart. 2 Chronicles 32:26

He humbles himself to speak to them.

To bring down; to lower; to reduce.

The highest mountains may be humbled into valleys.

To 'Humble' one's self, to repent; to afflict one's self for sin; to make contrite.

By the mid-nineteen hundreds, approximately 1956, the word 'Humble' is defined in the Webster's NEW TWENTIETH CENTURY Dictionary, Unabridged edition as:

Having or showing a consciousness of one's defects or shortcomings; not proud; not self-assertive; modest.

Low in condition, rank, or position; lowly; unimportant; unpretentious; as, a 'Humble' home.

To bring down; to lower in condition, rank or position; to abase; as, the power of Rome was humbled.

H = Humble---Chapter 11

"'Humble' yourselves therefore under the mighty hand of God, that He may exalt you in due time." 1 Peter 5:6 (KJV)

To be 'Humble' is to invite exaltation. (KS)

To make 'Humble' or lowly in mind; to abase the pride of; to reduce the arrogance and self-dependence of; in a religious sense, to make meek and submissive to the divine will: often used reflexively.
Synonyms---lowly, meek, submissive, unassuming, unobtrusive, unpretending…humiliate, lower, mortify, disgrace, degrade.

THAT'S IT!

Today, looking at a 1994 version of a students, Webster's New Dictionary the word 'Humble' is defined in <u>seven words only</u> as:
Not proud, lowly, modest, bring low, abase ... AND THIS IS SAD INDEED!

So Webster's Dictionary, since the day of Noah, has gone from two page definitions in 1828, to ¾ page definitions in 1956, to seven word definitions in 1994.

Continuing, being 'Humble', especially for males, is not always the easiest attribute, so I couldn't help but take advantage of the opportunity to define this chapter as detailed and clearly as possible.

I also wanted you to see the transition from 1828 until today to see for yourself how far we have come…or should I say fallen. Everything continues to be less in quantity, less in quality, and up in cost.

H = Humble---Chapter 11

"'Humble' yourselves therefore under the mighty hand of God, that He may exalt you in due time." 1 Peter 5:6 (KJV)
To be 'Humble' is to invite exaltation. (KS)

I say being truly 'Humble' is Christ like.

Paul shares with us in Philippians 2:8 (NIV) "And being found in appearance as a man, He humbled Himself and became obedient to death…even death on a cross!"

And Christ did this for us while we were yet sinners. And if we read on in V-9, as a result of His obedience, God exalted Him to the highest place and gave Him the name that is above every name.

Now today, I don't see our chances of having to die on a cross to prove our obedience as being very realistic, nor do I believe God is going to exalt any to the level of His Son, Jesus Christ. With that said, I do know that Jesus does make it quite clear in Matthew 23:12, "those who exalt themselves will be humbled, and those who humble themselves will be exalted," thus the reason for my quote at top of page, "*To be 'Humble' is to invite exaltation.*"

God knows if and when we give in secret, for the right reasons, and if and when we do so with a cheerful heart…and if done so begrudgingly.

For us to be 'Humble,' it must be unfeigned. We do not give to receive, but rather receive to give, as a sincere, natural and healthy instinct. Doing so, one might say we are living out 'Humble' ... walking the talk!

H = Humble---Chapter 11

"'Humble' yourselves therefore under the mighty hand of God, that He may exalt you in due time." 1 Peter 5:6 (KJV)

To be 'Humble' is to invite exaltation. (KS)

Another definition Noah used for 'Humble' was, "To 'Humble' one's self, to repent; to afflict one's self for sin; to make contrite."

To reach the level that Noah is speaking of, there needs to be a change of heart by way of a relationship with Jesus Christ. Only He has lived the experience to demonstrate being unfeignedly 'Humble'.

Noah is saying that we need to get down, mean and serious in regards to the sinful nature about us and clean up our act. We need to be deeply and thoroughly sorry for the sin we have committed, come clean and 'Humble' ourselves before God on our knees and by His mercy and grace be cleansed as white as snow, to be changed forever and to SIN NO MORE, as humanly, in the flesh, possible.

The sinful nature that entraps the unsaved soul is unable to achieve the humbleness as that of a soul touched by and led of God.
For an unsaved soul to profess they have humbled themselves as that of Christ is like saying that SOR'RY has the same impacting power as to 'Repent'.

It is literally a "ROYAL PRIVILEGE" for an individual to experience the true humbleness that only Christ can bestow upon them. As Peter says, noted at top, "'Humble' yourselves therefore under the mighty hand of God, that He may exalt you in due time." 1 Peter 5:6 (KJV)

BLACK & WHITE

Living life according to plan

H = Humble---Chapter 11

"'Humble' yourselves therefore under the mighty hand of God, that He may exalt you in due time." 1 Peter 5:6 (KJV)

To be 'Humble' is to invite exaltation. (KS)

Being ordained of God, to be 'Humble', is to gain also the willingness to understand patience… One might think of it as 'saintly patience.'

PATIENCE … He learnt with patience, and with meekness taught.
The suffering of afflictions, pain, toil, calamity, provocation or other evil, with a calm, unruffled temper; endurance without murmuring or fretfulness.

Patience may spring from constitutional fortitude, from a kind of heroic pride, or from Christian submission to the divine will. Being truly 'Humble' teaches us to be patient. As scripture reads in 2 Peter 3:8, "a day is like a thousand years to the Lord, and a thousand years is like a day." Our God is a patient God! (Romans 2:4)

Noah Webster once said of patience; "To tire in patience can mislead our sense."

Everyone knows that when we lose our patience, it never fails that we seem to lose all sense of what it was we were doing or going to do.
I used to train in martial arts and one of the key attributes was to have a 'Humble' and non-boastful spirit. In the act of self-defense the individual's ability to remain focused, calm and patient at all times can most assuredly give the upper hand.

H = Humble---Chapter 11

"'Humble' yourselves therefore under the mighty hand of God, that He may exalt you in due time." 1 Peter 5:6 (KJV)
To be 'Humble' is to invite exaltation. (KS)

To be 'Humble,' and still of this world, is like being one person on camera and another off. Yes, there are exceptions, but then we are back to seeing that being good, and being saved, do not mean the same thing. Being good does not take us to heaven; believing and being saved takes us to heaven.

Many churches today are teaching falsely that God is no longer a God of wrath but a loving and forgiving God who accepts and wraps His arms around everyone who does 'good'. This is clearly wrong and contrary to scripture; He does this yes, but expects full obedience to all His word.

God is very clear in Revelation 3 to the people of Laodicea that they were to be either for Him or against Him; otherwise, He was going to spit them out of His mouth. God is still a righteous, holy and forgiving God, but also a God of wrath if you do not repent of your ways and be reconciled back with Him through His Son, Jesus Christ; apart from Him we can do nothing (John 15:5).

To be 'Humble' in Christ is to be submissive to the divine will of God, our Creator…being a servant, 'Humble' and transparent and willing to give up all credit due for the glory of God and to those in our circle of influence such as family, friends, and peers. This is an unusual doctrine indeed to the ears of a selfish and proud world.

I = Inheritance---Chapter 12

To an inheritance incorruptible, and undefiled, and that fadeth not away, reserved in heaven for you. 1 Peter 1:4 (KJV)
Your 'Inheritance' has eternal value. (KS)

Do you know of anyone who has inherited anything from family, friends or unknown sources?

I recently heard of a young man who inherited approximately three quarters of a million dollars from a woman who had become like a second mom to him years prior from his hometown on the East Coast. This gift had come out of nowhere, because he had lost touch with this elderly woman for reasons unknown, but evidently, she hadn't forgotten him. Wow! That is unquestionably quite an 'Inheritance' to receive, let alone the surprise element attached.

You probably have a few stories to tell, and so do your friends and their friends, about gifts of perhaps less significant value, to the exuberant gifts that have shocked the recipients beyond all descriptive words of gratification.

Although said gifts hold deep meaning and much value, imagine if you can, a gift far more meaningful and valuable than any such gift you have ever received or could receive in your lifetime. Imagine a gift that could literally take you from dying to living forever...immortality...eternal life. Not Hollywood style...but for real! Not as in hokie-pokie ghost stories, wives tales or mythology, but real eternal life...closing our eyes here, better known as bodily/earthly death, and opening them up there, in paradise, better known as 'HEAVEN.'

I = Inheritance---Chapter 12

To an inheritance incorruptible, and undefiled, and that fadeth not away, reserved in heaven for you. 1 Peter 1:4 (KJV)

Your 'Inheritance' has eternal value. (KS)

So what's the catch? Jesus Christ, and there is no catch!

All you need to do is confess with your mouth that Jesus Christ is Lord…the Son of God…inviting Him to live inside of you as your personal Lord and Savior…believing wholeheartedly and without doubt that God our Heavenly Father, the Creator of all things, raised His Son from the dead…just like He promised He would do, and just like Jesus assured us He would do in the New Testament of the Holy Bible, … the bestselling book on the face of our planet year in and year out.

That's it! That's all that's needed to 'Inherit' eternal life.

If you confess with your mouth that Jesus is Lord and believe in your heart that God raised Him from the dead, you will be saved. (Romans 10:9 NIV)

YOUR 'INHERITANCE' IS ETERNAL LIFE WHEN YOU BELIEVE WITHOUT DOUBT THAT Jesus IS AS CLAIMED "I AND THE FATHER ARE ONE" (John 10:30).

Immediately following our confession, the Holy Spirit takes up residence in us and begins to change our heart; the way we think, the way we talk, and the path we follow as a sinner saved by grace.

BLACK & WHITE

Living life according to plan

I = Inheritance---Chapter 12

To an inheritance incorruptible, and undefiled, and that fadeth not away, reserved in heaven for you. 1 Peter 1:4 (KJV)

Your 'Inheritance' has eternal value. (KS)

For all have sinned and fall short of the glory of God, right, and because of our repentance, we are saved and eternal life is ours.

As Christians, we receive the 'Inheritance' of eternal life…and much, much more; guidance, wisdom, knowledge, understanding, integrity…and on and on the list goes.

Now that is worth getting excited about don't you think? And once you have received your 'Inheritance' no longer is it possible for man in any way, shape or form to steal back or kill your soul.

It is said," you can kill the body but you cannot kill the soul." (Matthew 10:28) Your soul, if you have sincerely acted on, Romans 10:9, has changed ownership from the devil, the prince of darkness, to the Prince of Peace, the King of Kings and the Lord of Lords.

You will recall me saying earlier on in chapter 2 that with Jesus Christ as your 'Overseer' you no longer have to carry the worries of the world, especially in concern to your eternal salvation.

Although you're not invincible to what the devil has in mind to draw you back into the sin of selfishness, deceit, lying, stealing, gossip, etcetera, you do however have the armor of God, which is the word of God as your defense, everything needed for a content and meaningful life.

BLACK & WHITE

Living life according to plan

I = Inheritance---Chapter 12

To an inheritance incorruptible, and undefiled, and that fadeth not away, reserved in heaven for you. 1 Peter 1:4 (KJV)

Your 'Inheritance' has eternal value. (KS)

So we can receive an 'Inheritance' of worldly value where moth and rust destroy and thieves break in and steal (Matthew 6:19-21) … or an 'Inheritance' of eternal life where death has been defeated on the cross by Jesus Christ, which is transferable to you upon placing your faith in Him. (John 3:16) I'm in…Amen!

I recall connecting via electronic mail with my cousin in California, a new Christian, and how she loved God…slowly discovering His amazing benefits, and at the same time, hopeful in prayer, to have the overflow of her new discoveries bless her husband and two boys as well, that they might join her for church services.

She says she invites all three each Sunday to join her, but while their answers remain mildly reluctant, she doesn't push and confidently leaves with the best love and patience in her heart possible, feeling confident God will fulfill her prayer request in His timing.

I share this because I see a driving force to receive the 'Inheritance' of eternal life in this particular case. Her mom, my aunt, passed away almost two years prior at the time of writing this, and not only did God place me in a position to lead my aunt through the sinners prayer of salvation, but also to deliver the eulogy at her funeral service.

I = Inheritance---Chapter 12

To an inheritance incorruptible, and undefiled, and that fadeth not away, reserved in heaven for you. 1 Peter 1:4 (KJV)

Your 'Inheritance' has eternal value. (KS)

My cousin received that message as God wanted her to, and as a result of that seed being planted, today her exact words via email reply were: "*There is no way in HELL that I am not going to spend eternity with my loving Mom and (Heavenly) FATHER!!!*" Love, G

The driving force was and is that my cousin heard of a way that would allow her to see her mom again, which meant asking Jesus Christ to help her believe, in order to accomplish this feat. Common sense led her to discover whether or not this unfamiliar territory of information was true. She has clearly shown that her search for answers is over and truth again prevails. Praise be to God for absolute truth alongside good old logic.

You have just read a perfect example of God at work, where He offered a message to a large audience, (at the funeral) and just one person, that we know of, took hold of that message, tested it, and can now say with understanding and confidence that one day she will share her gift of 'Inheritance' with her earthly mom as they live throughout eternity together. Does she have to understand it all? No! Is there any better answer available with evidence to back it up? No!

What about her family and extended family, guests and their friends? They were all in the very same room to hear the exact same message and to this day have yet to harness the simple truth they heard.

BLACK & WHITE

Living life according to plan

I = Inheritance---Chapter 12

To an inheritance incorruptible, and undefiled, and that fadeth not away, reserved in heaven for you. 1 Peter 1:4 (KJV)

Your 'Inheritance' has eternal value. (KS)

What about you and your family?

What better gift is there than the gift of defeating death as we know it?

What is it that keeps people from jumping all over this gift…especially when we are talking about 'FOREVER'? Does the word 'evil' come to mind?

May I be so bold in answering my own question by saying that there really is a devil, the prince of darkness, and his name is satan. He thrives on our weakness of disbelief of God, as well as pushing all areas of life itself, specializing in self deprivation and rushing us into the losers circle; satan's worldly manipulations are closer than one might think. Until we break those bonds and accept the fact and simple path of Christ, we will remain selfish, stubborn and ignorant of the very truth that will set us free.

Think of it! Choose Christ, find out it's a hoax and lose nothing--don't choose Christ, find out it's not a hoax and lose everything.

Just before presenting one final question for you to ponder, let me encourage you with this simple, 'black and white' analogy.

I = Inheritance---Chapter 12

To an inheritance incorruptible, and undefiled, and that fadeth not away, reserved in heaven for you. 1 Peter 1:4 (KJV)

Your 'Inheritance' has eternal value. (KS)

Satan is the promoter of everything unrighteous and ungodly including the likes of lying, cheating, adultery, stealing, thievery, all sexual immorality and perversion, witchcraft, hatred, idolatry, envy, drunkenness, and such. At birth, we are born into sin, the sinful nature of 'evil'.

People who support Secular Theocracy, often unknowingly and primarily out of human ignorance include the likes of Hitler, Stalin, Saddam Hussein, Ben Laden, and countless Hollywood celebrities, Presidential candidates, even the odd wavering Southern Baptist like Jesse Jackson; the list goes on and on; not judging, sharing!

Anyone, outside a relationship with Jesus Christ or who has attempted said relationship but chosen to add or take away from God's word found in Genesis 1:1 through Revelation 22:21, or who revels in idolatry, is guilty of supporting a theocracy other than true Christian Theocracy…and is indisputably bad news…although because of rights, often over right and wrong, are entitled to their own opinion…which I have no problem with.

THEOC'RACY, n. [Gr. God, and power; to hold.] Government of a state by the immediate direction of God; or the state thus governed.

I = Inheritance---Chapter 12

To an inheritance incorruptible, and undefiled, and that fadeth not away, reserved in heaven for you. 1 Peter 1:4 (KJV)
Your 'Inheritance' has eternal value. (KS)

IDOL'ATRY, n. [L. idololatria. Gr. idol, and to worship or serve.]...The worship of idols, images, or any, thing, made by hands, or which is not of God -- Definitions from: Webster's 1828 Dictionary

What I mean by bad news, above, is that in God's world, He offers us two choices ...For Him or Against Him, believe or don't believe. There are consequences and He describes clearly, both Heaven and Hell.

We cannot serve two masters! In Matthew 6:24 Jesus tells us: ... "No one can serve two masters. For you will hate one and love the other, or be devoted to one and despise the other." As an example, we cannot say we are Christian one minute and support same-sex marriage or abortion the next. Both of these issues undisputedly defy God's word...

...Or we cannot say we are Christian while believing in the likes of scientology or any other ideology...which is idolatry...where your treasure is, so your heart will be also...

...Or we cannot be instilling fear and hate and murdering innocent people and consider ourselves as a loving person at the same time...we either love like Christ or we don't.

We live in a world with two sides to it. We inherit eternal life through absolute truth or we do not. Clearer still, in our world there is 'GOOD' and there is 'EVIL'; evil exists where God does not.

BLACK & WHITE

Living life according to plan

I = Inheritance---Chapter 12

To an inheritance incorruptible, and undefiled, and that fadeth not away, reserved in heaven for you. 1 Peter 1:4 (KJV)

Your 'Inheritance' has eternal value. (KS)

Good is God…and evil is satan! If we are not for God then that leaves us in an unfavorable position, and our freedom is one or the other.

Now God on the other hand is the promoter of everything contrary to the above, creating all righteousness and everything truthful, holy, divine-design-marriage and family, values and morals.

People who support Christian Theocracy may include: Billy Graham, D. L. Moody, Mother Teresa, and our converted Jewish friends including, Abraham, Isaac, Jacob, Noah, Moses, David, Ruth, Mary and Mary Magdalene, Matthew, Mark, Luke, John and Paul, being a handful of 40+ biblical authors; all of whom, like everyone of the flesh, the furthest thing from perfect...apart from Christ who was perfect and sin-free.

The common denominator with all of these individuals is having a personal relationship with our Savior, Jesus Christ. The power of the Holy Spirit is inherited within each Christian worldwide, guiding all to do the goodness and the will of our Heavenly Father, the Creator of all things, in heaven, on earth and below the earth, and doing so, to the best of our ability as sinners saved by grace.

One might believe in 'once saved always saved' while another may disagree…one might believe more strongly in serving while another more firmly in evangelism. But each focus is rock solid in the Christian

I = Inheritance---Chapter 12

To an inheritance incorruptible, and undefiled, and that fadeth not away, reserved in heaven for you. 1 Peter 1:4 (KJV)
Your 'Inheritance' has eternal value. (KS)

faith and supported by text in the Holy Bible, without adding or taking away from God's word. Just as we can agree to disagree on pieces of God's text, while both opinions are within God's word, so it is as well that each of us has our own unique gifts, thanks be to God, some of us are granted special gifts, again, by the power of the Holy Spirit; 1 Corinthians 12:7-11 is an example of the latter.

We can agree to disagree when an interpretational difference lies within scripture, with both sides having a viable claim grounded in God's word. The Deity of Christ, is however, an absolute truth that is not up for negotiation; Jesus Christ is the Son of God--God in the flesh, as proclaimed in John 10:30.

We've identified that there is 'GOOD' and there is 'EVIL' in our world. We've seen that 'GOOD' is of God and that 'EVIL' is of satan. We've also seen that if we are not for God, then that means we must be against Him, no in-between, even though we might see ourselves as a good person; let us simply and logically justify that now.

When Eve and then Adam sinned, we were immediately separated from our all-righteous, holy and sovereign God, Creator, for eternity. Sin entered the world and we inherited death as we know it today; and there is only one way for man to restore that relationship with God.

BLACK & WHITE
Living life according to plan

I = Inheritance---Chapter 12

To an inheritance incorruptible, and undefiled, and that fadeth not away, reserved in heaven for you. 1 Peter 1:4 (KJV)

Your 'Inheritance' has eternal value. (KS)

Jesus Christ died on the cross, was buried, and raised from the dead, as the perfect, unblemished sacrifice for the sins of all man. (See: 2 Corinthians 5:21, Hebrews 4:15, Hebrews 7:26-27, 1 John 3:5)

Every sin ever committed, and to be committed, in the world was taken upon the shoulders of Christ as He defeated death on the cross. We are saved through the cross and 'Him' crucified, and His resurrection.

When we believe this, confessing it with our mouth that Jesus is Lord and believe in our hearts that God raised Him from the dead, confessing our sins and asking for forgiveness, we will be saved, defeating death as we know it and inheriting eternal life (Romans 10:9).

Until that day, when we are once again connected back with God, through Christ, we remain an enemy of God, as unbelievers. Yes He loves all, but as an all righteous, holy and sovereign God, He has given us the freedom of choice, free will, to believe or not to believe. Once again…we are either for Him or we are against him.

So what about you? Will you believe or not believe? Is eternal life, the comfort of knowing you can live without fear of dying (*death to the body not the soul*), with high expectations of what comes next, important to you? Are you willing to risk it all, allowing the evil inherited from birth to take control of your eternal destination?

BLACK & WHITE

Living life according to plan

I = Inheritance---Chapter 12

To an inheritance incorruptible, and undefiled, and that fadeth not away, reserved in heaven for you. 1 Peter 1:4 (KJV)

Your 'Inheritance' has eternal value. (KS)

Are you willing to take the word of the one who stands for nothing but absolute evil…who has demonstrated his kind of world intention through the likes of Hitler or Saddam Hussein, Margaret Sanger, or the likes of Islamic Extremists/*al-Qaeda,* today...who implants deception and fear into the minds of every man, woman and child, while diminishing all true value as meaningless, and all while impregnating the mind that today is the only thing that's important?

…OR…

Will you step out in faith long enough to uncover absolute truth that is found only in He who has remained unchanged from the beginning of time…who has repeatedly shown all the goodness of His world intentions by way of His promises and plans for you…by way of His creations such as the flowers and the mountains, to the conception and birth of a child, to the human brain that surpasses all created design, effort and understanding…to the unforgettable efforts of individuals like Mother Teresa and Billy Graham or such marvelous organizations as 'The Salvation Army'? When disaster strikes, who's there; Christians in droves, right! He gives us a choice and we are either one or the other.

Being an unbeliever is certainly the easiest path to take because it comes with no responsibility or effort attached, nor is there need to confess or recognize our sins. We can just do as we please.

BLACK & WHITE

Living life according to plan

I = Inheritance---Chapter 12

To an inheritance incorruptible, and undefiled, and that fadeth not away, reserved in heaven for you. 1 Peter 1:4 (KJV)

Your 'Inheritance' has eternal value. (KS)

What we need to appreciate, is that we cannot be a party animal, be ignorant and disrespectful of our spouse and others, go around disobeying the laws, cursing and swearing, cheating, lying, being full of pride or the likes, and still be right with our maker; *conviction is a good thing and that is what the Holy Spirit does to us when we get off course*.

With Christ the old self is left behind (2 Corinthians 5:17). Does this mean we must live as prudes? No! Quite the contrary! We simply spend our days as anyone else but striving to be the best we can be, avoiding, and if not completely, our need for indulging in excessive alcohol, taking un-prescribed drugs, substance abuse, etcetera and etcetera. A true Christian is one who realizes they are not perfect, and chooses to improve by setting an example that loves all, judges none, while striving to be the best we can be.

Even if we feel confident as a person who is always doing 'good' and causing no one harm, we are still guilty of the hidden, inner and un-confessed sin that is born of us all. Christ died for all seen and unseen sin, and unless we accept what He has done, by faith, we cannot and will not inherit heaven nor the fringe benefits of eternal life to come.

Let's think about this for a moment! We inherit ignorance (sin) as part of our evil shell from birth, no exceptions, like it or not, which is why we struggle to humble ourselves to seek and accept absolute truth.

I = Inheritance---Chapter 12

To an inheritance incorruptible, and undefiled, and that fadeth not away, reserved in heaven for you. 1 Peter 1:4 (KJV)

Your 'Inheritance' has eternal value. (KS)

On the other hand, we can capitalize on the humble assistance needed to accept absolute truth, by simply inviting Christ to lead our lives, as our personal Lord and Savior, thus, inheriting eternal life and defeating death, which puts the ball back in our court. How's that for a game changer?

Now common sense comes into play here, even if we think that we are already a good person and that we don't need Christ in our lives. Meaning, if not accepting Christ into our lives leaves us in partnership with the evil side of life, the devil himself (See Galatians 5:16-26 / 2 Timothy 3:1-5), but, by accepting Christ, catapults us to the good side of life, with God, front-row-center, receiving the 'Inheritance' of heaven and all its rewards, what do you suppose is the logical choice?

So you say, "I will think about it and maybe decide tomorrow." What if tomorrow never comes? Or you say, I'll make a decision by next Friday, but what if next Friday never comes?

HELLO! … I'm 1% clowning and 99% serious here.

My friend, your eternal 'Inheritance' is awaiting you, so don't put off to tomorrow what you can do today. Eternity is a long, long time.

T = Thanksgiving---Chapter 13

Blessing, and glory, and wisdom, and thanksgiving, and honour, and power, and might, *be* unto our God for ever and ever. Rev 7:12 (KJV)

Our 'Thanksgiving' is due Him daily. (KS)

Noah Webster's defined 'Thanksgiving' as,

The act of rendering thanks or expressing gratitude for favors or mercies…
A public celebration of divine goodness … [The practice of appointing an annual thanksgiving originated in New England.]
A day set apart for religious services, especially to acknowledge the goodness of God, either in regards to deliverance from calamities or danger, or in the ordinary dispensation of his bounties…

David says in Psalm 100 … (The Psalm of 'Thanksgiving')

1 Shout with joy to the Lord, O earth! 2 Worship the Lord with gladness.
Come before him, singing with joy. 3 Acknowledge that the Lord is God!
He made us, and we are his. We are his people, the sheep of his pasture.
4 Enter his gates with 'Thanksgiving'; go into his courts with praise.
Give thanks to him and bless his name. 5 For the Lord is good. His
unfailing love continues forever, and his faithfulness continues to each
generation.

If there was ever just one reason to give thanks, then I'd say we found it in John 3:16 that says; "*For God so loved the world that he gave his only Son, so that everyone who believes in him will not perish but have eternal life.*"

T = Thanksgiving---Chapter 13

Blessing, and glory, and wisdom, and thanksgiving, and honour, and power, and might, *be* unto our God for ever and ever. Rev 7:12 (KJV)
Our 'Thanksgiving' is due Him daily. (KS)

How many soldiers over the course of two world wars, and countless others in between, died in the line of fire for the cause, or as the result of saving the life of a fellow comrade? God knows each by name.

Countless soldiers who died for another are all acts of true heroism unquestionably. They died so their friends might live. They died so that peace and freedom might be spread throughout the world; not a time and place to discuss the politics/propaganda of war...but you hear me!

Every individual that dies in a war, whether intentionally to save a comrades life or for the unknown falsified cause, are all remembered as heroes and brave ones at that. Those like me who have never experienced anything of the sort can never take lightly what must have transpired in the minds of those brave men and woman moments before death nor those who survived only to be plagued lifelong by the inner haunting.

I'm thankful for Remembrance Day Services around the world. In comparison to the sacrifices made, it's a small but important way for us to remember and acknowledge all those brave veterans.

Now let us consider a thanksgiving that surpasses all sacrificed for the sake of all people on all four quarters of the earth.

BLACK & WHITE

Living life according to plan

T = Thanksgiving---Chapter 13

Blessing, and glory, and wisdom, and thanksgiving, and honour, and power, and might, *be* unto our God for ever and ever. Rev 7:12 (KJV)

Our 'Thanksgiving' is due Him daily. (KS)

Jesus Christ also died for His comrades! He went somewhat further and died on a cross for you, the world, and I, so that we might have life more abundantly. That is the elite of 'Thanksgiving.'

Jesus was the unblemished lamb needed to die on a cross, shouldering every sin ever committed or to be committed by a sinful world. We are not talking about giving His life to save the life of one, two or a squadron of fellow comrades, a most honorable and noble thing to do, but rather, about a divine purpose and reason for dying, so that, upon our individual asking, our sin and all sin committed, could be washed away, leaving us white as snow, as though said sin never existed.

God shows no favoritism (1 Peter 1:17). 'The Son of Sam, Jack the Ripper, the guilty drunk driver, the child molester, the drug addict, the thief, the sexually immoral, the curser, the adulterer, the idolater, the selfish, the proud, or the arrogant, as mere examples, only need to ask Jesus Christ to forgive them of their sins, invite Him into the driver's seat of their lives to take care of their specific problem and it's a done deal. Again, that to me is the elite of all 'Thanksgiving.'

Noah Webster used a rather fitting phrase for Christ in describing Him as being 'thank-worthy'… deserving thanks or meritorious.

BLACK & WHITE

Living life according to plan

T = Thanksgiving---Chapter 13

Blessing, and glory, and wisdom, and thanksgiving, and honour, and power, and might, *be* unto our God for ever and ever. Rev 7:12 (KJV)

Our 'Thanksgiving' is due Him daily. (KS)

The word 'meritorious' is described as; 'Deserving of reward or of notice, regard, fame or happiness, or of that which shall be a suitable return for services or excellence of any kind.' Noah completed, "*we rely for salvation on the meritorious obedience and sufferings of Christ.*"

Let us consider Paul, formerly known as Saul, and persecutor of Christ, and what he said to us in 2 Corinthians 4:14-15 … 14 We know that the same God who raised our Lord Jesus will also raise us with Jesus and present us to himself along with you. 15 All of these things are for your benefit. And as God's grace brings more and more people to Christ, there will be great 'Thanksgiving', and God will receive more and more glory.

This my friend, is what God is all about, and He loves to receive more and more of the glory, and rightfully so. He could have discarded our filthy deserving souls forever, during or after, the Genesis flood, but He had mercy on an undeserving people and chose to establish an everlasting covenant with Noah, on our behalf for our benefit.

In Genesis 9:13-17 (NKJ) we read, 13 "I set My rainbow in the cloud, and it shall be for the sign of the covenant between Me and the earth. 14 It shall be, when I bring a cloud over the earth, that the rainbow shall be seen in the cloud; 15 and I will remember My covenant which is between Me and you and every living creature of all flesh; the waters shall never again become a flood to destroy all flesh.

T = Thanksgiving---Chapter 13

Blessing, and glory, and wisdom, and thanksgiving, and honour, and power, and might, *be* unto our God for ever and ever. Rev 7:12 (KJV)

Our 'Thanksgiving' is due Him daily. (KS)

...16 The rainbow shall be in the cloud, and I will look on it to remember the everlasting covenant between God and every living creature of all flesh that is on the earth." 17 And God said to Noah, "This is the sign of the covenant which I have established between Me and all flesh that is on the earth."

From the time we open our eyes in the morning to the time we close them at night we must admit it, 'Thanksgiving' is a mere pittance compared to what Christ has done, is doing, and will continue doing, for us while we were yet sinners (Romans 5:8).

We wake up every morning undeservingly! For all have sinned and fall short of the glory of God (Romans 3:23), and though I too am a sinner saved by grace, I also am still unworthy to expect that a holy and righteous God should be giving me the time of day. But He does, because HE is a humble, all loving, understanding and compassionate God full of goodness, mercy and forgiveness, eager to shower us with endless love and blessings, and all in return for mere obedience.

How about our senses? He has blessed us with the gift to listen, taste, touch, smell, and sight, that we might see everything before us; beside us, behind us or around us, each and every moment of every day.

T = Thanksgiving---Chapter 13

Blessing, and glory, and wisdom, and thanksgiving, and honour, and power, and might, *be* unto our God for ever and ever. Rev 7:12 (KJV)
Our 'Thanksgiving' is due Him daily. (KS)

Consider, day and night, the sun, moon, stars, the clouds, the rain…you get the picture! We could live on earth forever and never see all that He has made and provided us, graciously and freely.

I live in Eastern Ontario Canada where we are blessed with the autumn season every year that is truly magnificent. To watch the maple tree go through its natural transition of plush green to numerous colors such as orange, yellow, red, burgundy or of multiple brilliance is, at times, beyond what words can describe; and still, once a tree always a tree.

In an article published by Agape Press, http://www.agapepress.org dated November 22, 2004, the Reverend Mark H. Creech, executive director of the Christian Action League of North Carolina, Inc. calact@aol.com quoted, Cicero, as saying: "*Gratitude is not only the greatest of virtues but also the parent of all the others*." He concluded, that he couldn't agree more with the great philosopher, but if thankfulness was at the heart of all virtue, then certainly thanklessness was the mother of all sins.

Rev. Mark goes on to write:
[Today, America has a population in excess of three hundred million people. We produce more than any other nation in the world. The median family income is $50,000 annually. In a time of war, God has given us victory over our enemies. Yet we are so unthankful.

T = Thanksgiving---Chapter 13

Blessing, and glory, and wisdom, and thanksgiving, and honour, and power, and might, *be* unto our God for ever and ever. Rev 7:12 (KJV)

Our 'Thanksgiving' is due Him daily. (KS)

At this time of the year, real thankfulness could be the turn-about our nation desperately needs. Luke 24:13-33 tells the remarkable story of how Jesus appeared after His resurrection to two men on their way to Emmaus. They had hoped Jesus was the promised Messiah who would redeem Israel. But their hopes have been dashed since Jesus was crucified and even His body now appeared to be stolen. Feeling distraught, perplexed and defeated, they didn't recognize Jesus as He came alongside to walk with them down that dusty road. As they arrived at Emmaus during eventide, they prepared to partake of a meal together. Still a stranger to them, Jesus lifted up His voice in 'Thanksgiving' as He broke bread. It was in that moment, the Bible says, "*their eyes were opened*" and joy filled their hearts. They realized Jesus was not dead, but risen, alive and present with them. It's profoundly significant that they recognized our Lord in the act of 'Thanksgiving'. 'Thanksgiving' opens the way to the presence of God.] …End

God is everything good. It is He who humbles us to the point of understanding and appreciating the need to give thanks. He humbles the proud and exalts the meek. It is He that instituted all virtue…ordaining thankfulness of God, leaving thanklessness as the root or as mentioned previously, the mother of all sin.

The song 'Give Thanks' copyright 1978 with Integrity Hosanna Music, says it well:

BLACK & WHITE
Living life according to plan

T = Thanksgiving---Chapter 13

Blessing, and glory, and wisdom, and thanksgiving, and honour, and power, and might, *be* unto our God for ever and ever. Rev 7:12 (KJV)

Our 'Thanksgiving' is due Him daily. (KS)

[Give thanks with a grateful heart
Give thanks to the Holy one
Give thanks because He's given Jesus Christ His son
And now, let the weak say I am strong, let the poor say I am rich because of what the Lord has done for us.]

Our 'Thanksgiving' is most reverently due Him daily.

Evangelist Billy Graham once said, "Ingratitude is a sin, just as surely as is lying or stealing or immorality or any other sin condemned by the Bible." www.rbc.net (Our Daily Bread 11/25/04 devotion)

In the book of Romans 1:21 we read, "Yes, they knew God, but they wouldn't worship him as God or even give him thanks. And they began to think up foolish ideas of what God was like. The result was that their minds became dark and confused."

*** Allow me to expand on this for a moment with a little head game: *** If we were to take the 1 as in Romans 1 and then add the 2 and the 1 as in verse 21, (1+2+1) it would total "4"…And if we would think of verse 21 as being the 21st Century, and the total "4" as the fourth year (2004)…to our surprise, Romans 1:21 above, fits perfectly with where we are today as a society does it not?

T = Thanksgiving---Chapter 13

Blessing, and glory, and wisdom, and thanksgiving, and honour, and power, and might, *be* unto our God for ever and ever. Rev 7:12 (KJV)

Our 'Thanksgiving' is due Him daily. (KS)

Now as strange and preposterous as this wild and off the wall mind-maze may appear, it really does fit with November 28, 2004, @ 2200hs to be exact, as I'm writing this part of the book. Today (10+ years ago now), anything and everything is acceptable and negotiable except the truth…with no signs of slowing down.

Billy Graham also said; "Nothing turns us into bitter, selfish, dissatisfied people more quickly than an ungrateful heart. And nothing will do more to restore contentment and the joy of our salvation than a true spirit of thankfulness." (Our Daily Bread 11/25/04 devotion)

'Thanksgiving' for me is an opportunity to give thanks for what I don't have, because our possessions turn us into the people we become and I might not like another kind of me.

'Thanksgiving' for me is a time to give thanks for everything I do have, for too many others have far less than I.

'Thanksgiving' for me is also a time to give thanks for what is yet to come, for everything is from God, and if I deserve it, I'll receive it.

What is 'Thanksgiving' for you? What are you thankful for? When did you thank God last for all you have in your life? Have you considered giving thanks for what you don't have, or what's to come?

T = Thanksgiving---Chapter 13

Blessing, and glory, and wisdom, and thanksgiving, and honour, and power, and might, *be* unto our God for ever and ever. Rev 7:12 (KJV)

Our 'Thanksgiving' is due Him daily. (KS)

I heard a story recently where a visiting Pastor was in a school handing out free pens to a grade five class and as he went about the room distributing the pens, it wasn't until he had reached the twelfth child, did he receive a 'thank you.' How sad is that!

Might I encourage you to add 'thank you' to the top of your daily to-do-list? Not only is it the courteous and respectful thing to do, but also and more importantly, gratitude is a God-honoring attitude and our Creator first and foremost, is deserving of our 'Thanksgiving.'

"I am the Alpha and the Omega—the beginning and the end," says the Lord God. "I am the one who is, who always was, and who is still to come, the Almighty One." Revelation 1:8 (NLT)
All I said was, "I believe you are real, come into my life and change it, and He did." (KS)

Endnote

One of the toughest issues I dealt with in my attempt to learn more of God was that I didn't enjoy reading. I was slower than most, an average student, yet consistently and genuinely intrigued with learning. Even if I couldn't have read at all, there were other learning methods such as audio, video, and even Braille, amen, in countless languages.

If there was a higher power, evidenced by looking around us, then I would need to read if I was to know how to secure my soul for eternal rest. And the only bible I had was a gift from my Grama Hogan, received on December 25, 1966, that was full of Thou's and Thee's and morrow's and therein's etc. This was a bit overwhelming for me.

After discovering that bibles could be purchased in many different translations (not versions), I picked up my own New International Version (NIV) that read almost like everyday conversation. I then grounded myself in a bible believing and teaching church and quickly discovered that God was far more than what I had expected or could have imagined.

I then needed to discover for myself other religions available.

BLACK & WHITE

Living life according to plan

"I am the Alpha and the Omega—the beginning and the end," says the Lord God. "I am the one who is, who always was, and who is still to come, the Almighty One." Revelation 1:8 (NLT)

All I said was, "I believe you are real, come into my life and change it, and He did." (KS)

Endnote

So I began looking into the likes of, Mormonism, Jehovah's Witnesses, Islam, Scientology, New Age, Hindu, Buddhism, and Judaism etcetera, but quickly discovered the all too common denominator in each and every one of them, but Christianity…Man!

Divine accomplishment (the living God), was the missing common denominator. Instead I found the world to be full of man and his pride and human accomplishment called religion. Judaism was claiming the same God as the Christian faith, but appeared to be missing the part where the good had gotten much better with a Savior included…Old Testament (1st Covenant) to the New Testament (2nd Covenant).

This was mind boggling to a novice like myself, considering the Old Testament addresses countless and deliberate references to the coming Messiah, our much needed Savior…And my Bible identifies these promises fulfilled via the New Testament, in every detail.

As for the 'religions,' per se, one doesn't need to be a rocket scientist to see that they are founded on the wisdom of man, not from the living God. In addition, they cannot provide us scientific and/or archaeological discoveries in support of their claims, including Hollywood's 'Scientology' as nothing more than man eager for answers.

"I am the Alpha and the Omega—the beginning and the end," says the Lord God. "I am the one who is, who always was, and who is still to come, the Almighty One." Revelation 1:8 (NLT)
All I said was, "I believe you are real, come into my life and change it, and He did." (KS)

Endnote

Evidence continues to stack up in favor of the Christian faith daily by way of answered prayer, countless testimonies and numerous unbiased authors and/or their websites in support of what is found within the pages of the Holy Bible, Genesis 1:1 - Revelation 22:21…all 31,173 verses.

So here I am a good number of years later, an unknown author, Pastor and Speaker with another book, "BLACK & WHITE!" which is the first of a three book series entitled, "Challenged by Default."

Thank you for being here! Thank you for reading my books. I trust this particular book has encouraged you to take the next step that God wants you to take. He has big plans for you and I am honored to have had the opportunity to play a small part in that journey.

You're now ready for God's four-step formula, the second book of this series entitled, "God, *self,* Family and Career," that will be available soon, if not already. He (God) can now assist you in unraveling the confusion as to what needs to come first, and answering some of the most commonly asked questions, such as:

"I am the Alpha and the Omega—the beginning and the end," says the Lord God. "I am the one who is, who always was, and who is still to come, the Almighty One." Revelation 1:8 (NLT)

All I said was, "I believe you are real, come into my life and change it, and He did." (KS)

Endnote

"How can I tithe 10% to God when He needs to be first in my life, and yet unable to feed my family without a job?"…OR…"God does not pay the bills in my house, I do, so why wouldn't my career be number one, so I can tithe and also feed my family and perhaps give to God's purposes at that time?"

The third book of this series, "Challenged by Default" as mentioned, is also the title of said series … It will identify our weaknesses, why we have them, plus, show us how to improve and monitor our integral character. PS: My book, 'The New You,' also addresses this issue.

God has been good to me with each book in this series and I'm extremely grateful that He has provided me with such a simplistic style for delivering His truth to you and thousands of others across His awesome universe. He enables me to keep a simple message simple, as need be.

Allow me now to wish you enjoyable reading and learning, and encourage you to never stop growing in His word. God is good all the time, literally, and only He can resolve our issues and struggles in life, if we are willing to hand it over to him 100%; not 50%, not 75%, but 100% of the time, all the time.

BLACK & WHITE

Living life according to plan

"I am the Alpha and the Omega—the beginning and the end," says the Lord God. "I am the one who is, who always was, and who is still to come, the Almighty One." Revelation 1:8 (NLT)

All I said was, "I believe you are real, come into my life and change it, and He did." (KS)

Endnote - close

Interesting quote: *We can have masses of wealth or live in a makeshift underground shack, but both have one thing in common...Spiritual bankruptcy unless we have Jesus Christ*--author unknown

I am inspired daily by the courage of all who strive to find the answer to their most crucial question, "Where will I spend eternity?" Very wise!

I believe this book has more than pointed you in the right direction, to end up in the right place when your last breath is taken on this earth. (HINT: John 3:16).

God is good my friend! Continue to place your trust in Him; The Father, The Son and The Holy Spirit, [The Holy Trinity].

May you, your family, and all you do be blessed abundantly!

Live and love the life He offers,

Kevin
wearenotgod@gmail.com
www.wearenotgod.com

A few keeper quotes

The difference between what we think we want and what our true purpose really is often a matter of quieting ourselves long enough to listen; start here! James 1:19—Kevin Simpson

There is one thing that is certain and perfect in our universe PLUS one thing that is certain and imperfect; the One who created all we see, and those created to maintain it—Kevin Simpson

Decisions = determined destiny *** Decisions following good, experience related counsel = refined destiny *** Decisions under the Will of God = absolute destiny—Kevin Simpson

To say we are sorry is like saying 'whoops!' To repent is to regret inappropriate selfish action and being determined to change the heart accordingly, with the help and grace of God—Kevin Simpson

The difference between being in the top 20% or the top 1% at anything we do is simply being EXTRAordinary—Kevin Simpson

Judging another is the result of self-discontentment; love self, love thy neighbor—Kevin Simpson

We have all played cover-up—but noticed or unnoticed, confessing it is wise—Kevin Simpson

Win/Win works in relationships, business and life without excuse—Kevin Simpson

Being forgiven and being unforgiving is a two way story on a one way street—Kevin Simpson

A few keeper quotes

There really are still people in the world who care to achieve nothing of great significance, unless they can take others with them; that person will be one after God's own heart—Kevin Simpson

EMPATHY: Take self out of the equation, put another's problems on the line, and you get an earth shattering result; people moving mountains, previously immoveable, all because they first, helped someone else move a mountain of their own—Kevin Simpson

We must become less to become one of the best; *the greatest servant is the one who serves the best not the one looking to be served*—Kevin Simpson

Better to be gossiped about than the one doing the gossip—Kevin Simpson

Our track record will come to our rescue a time or two in the future; *for the good or the bad will remain to be seen*—Kevin Simpson

When men lose the courage to face what they fear, they lose what they desire; *God created us and wants only the best for us, therefore, running to Him and not from Him is wise*—Kevin Simpson

Every situation and predicament in life is invaluable for those who choose to capitalize on every moment of learning God provides us—Kevin Simpson

The word 'inferior' is merely one more word the devil chooses to favor in his attempt to keep us as far away as possible from the absolute truth and love of Jesus Christ—Kevin Simpson

A few keeper quotes

God, in His infinite wisdom and graciousness has provided each of us unlimited ability to achieve our fill of unselfishly motivated desires; *our only hindrance is called OBEDIENCE*—Kevin Simpson

Let us not be so caught up in achievement that we forget to live and miss appreciating what we have; *content with little or much makes for a wise person*—Kevin Simpson

Just as bad news travels light years faster than good, so it is with a blemished character; *protect it ever so dearly*—Kevin Simpson

True integrity might be described as unselfish character firmly grounded in moral, ethical, and accountable values; *follow Christ and so shall it be*—Kevin Simpson

We are all capable of so much more…and then some…so why wait—Kevin Simpson

To continue learning is to stay young, wise, and more importantly, on the right path; *following Christ (Creator) first, not man (created) first*—Kevin Simpson

Made in the USA
Charleston, SC
28 February 2016